Twentieth Century
Interpretations

THE GRAPES
OF WRATH

A Collection of Critical Essays

Edited by
ROBERT CON DAVIS

Prentice-Hall, Inc. A SPECTRUM BOOK *Englewood Cliffs, N.J. 07632*

Library of Congress Cataloging in Publication Data
Main entry under title:

The grapes of wrath.

(Twentieth Century Interpretations) "A Spectrum Book."
   Bibliography: p.
   1. Steinbeck, John, 1902–1963. The grapes of
   wrath—Addresses, essays, lectures.   I. Davis,
   Robert Con, 1948–
   PS3537.T3234G734   1982   813'.52   81-19993
                                                      AACR2

ISBN 0-13-363358-6

ISBN 0-13-363341-1 {PBK.} 813.5209
                          DS8192

This Spectrum Book is available to businesses and organizations
at a special discount when ordered in large quantities. For
information, contact Prentice-Hall, Inc., General Publishing
Division, Special Sales, Englewood Cliffs, N.J. 07632.

Prentice-Hall International, Inc., *London*
Prentice-Hall of Australia Pty. Limited, *Sydney*
Prentice-Hall of Canada, Ltd., *Toronto*
Prentice-Hall of India Private Limited, *New Delhi*
Prentice-Hall of Japan, Inc., *Tokyo*
Prentice-Hall of Southeast Asia Pte. Ltd., *Singapore*
Whitehall Books Limited, *Wellington, New Zealand*

*This book is dedicated to Elva Covene Anderson,
my mother, who also made the difficult trip
from Oklahoma to California.*

Contents

Part One—Interpretations

Part Two—Viewpoints

Acknowledgments

I wish to thank my colleagues Robert Murray Davis and Ronald Schleifer for their help as I assembled this collection. They both read and criticized the Introduction, to my great benefit. Robert Murray Davis, in particular, gave his expert advice on Steinbeck scholarship and in other ways helped as experts generally can. Also, I am indebted to my students at the University of Oklahoma, especially David Moore, for their helpful questions *and* insights. And I would like to thank Melanie Ruth Collins for her assistance with the collection and for her helpful editing.

Introduction

by Robert Con Davis

In a recent study of John Steinbeck's work, Peter Lisca ends an introductory paragraph on *The Grapes of Wrath* as follows:

> Although thus associated with this class of social-protest fiction *The Grapes of Wrath* continues to be read, not as a piece of literary or social history, but with a sense of emotional involvement and aesthetic discovery. More than any other American novel, it successfully embodies a contemporary social problem of national scope in an artistically viable expression. It is unquestionably John Steinbeck's finest achievement, a work of literary genius.[1]

Lisca conveys the spirit if not the precise letter of current sentiment about *The Grapes of Wrath*. The novel is clearly Steinbeck's best work; it is an important and influential novel—possibly, as Lisca claims, "a work of literary genius." And yet one who approaches it for the first time, or who is just beginning to study it closely, may not readily understand why it is important—or may not even know exactly *how* to read it. Its reception among students in my modern literature courses suggests that contemporary readers with a grasp of Richard Brautigan, Hunter S. Thompson, and Thomas Pynchon are not necessarily prepared to read Steinbeck—at least not to understand him. Why? Can *The Grapes of Wrath* be difficult? To think of it in that way is startling. Yet just as Lionel Trilling found it necessary to explain the "difficulties" of William Dean Howells, so now readers may need to be introduced to the "difficulties" of *The Grapes of Wrath*. That is, they may need to retrieve the sensibility for reading it well in a way that did not seem necessary only a short time ago. Contemporary readers may now need to study *The Grapes of Wrath*, because this novel—though recently a work of contemporary fiction—stands

[1]For this passage, see the essay by Lisca in this collection.

now, we must recall, in the middle distance of American literary history.

Central for understanding *The Grapes of Wrath* is the recognition that it runs counter to one of the main developments in twentieth-century American literature—modernist fiction. From the belated "discovery" of *Moby-Dick* in the early part of this century to recent experiments, there has been a strong revisionist and experimental tradition in American writing, producing fiction as diverse as that of John Dos Passos, William Faulkner, and Thomas Pynchon—fiction that often appears to erode settled novelistic practices to discover new literary forms. Readers know this tradition by its rejection of the authority of the past, its willingness to experiment with genre, its belief in multiplicity (as opposed to unity) of meaning, and its rejection of romantic sentiment. *The Grapes of Wrath,* as Warren French has noted,[2] stands apart from all this, having no serious quarrel with the past, no especially innovative or experimental form, no obsession with multiplicity or ambiguity, and no fear of sentiment. Accordingly, a reader may judge Steinbeck's novel to be optimistic about society and affirmative about the human spirit in depicting the Joad family's successful struggle to cross the country, Tom Joad's and Jim Casy's meditation on the social and spiritual changes around them, and Rose of Sharon's impulse to nurse a starving world. If these depictions have a quaint look to us, it is not because they belong to another era and are irrelevant to ours, but because they are foreign to the critical idiom that dominates the twentieth century. They do not show the influence of modernism.

On this account, from 1939 to 1954, during what Peter Lisca calls the "hysterical reaction" to the novel, many readers tended to classify *The Grapes of Wrath* as a social document with only marginal literary status.[3] Malcolm Cowley and Joseph Warren Beach defended the novel's integrity, proclaiming it an achievement of artistic vision; but Kenneth Burke, Edmund Wilson, and Frederic J. Hoffman saw in it a dishonest novel—a novel propagandistic in its appeal. Alfred Kazin—uniquely taking both sides—called it "the most influential social novel of the period," but simultaneously

---

[2]"Presidential Message: Steinbeck and Modernism," *Steinbeck Quarterly,* 8, 3 and 4 (Summer-Fall 1976): 69–71.

[3]In "The Pattern of Criticism," Peter Lisca, ed., *The Grapes of Wrath* (New York: Viking Press, 1972), p. 695.

complained of a lack of realism in its characters.[4] In the view of many, the migration from Oklahoma and the trials of those who left their homes were presented too directly, as if to win readers' sympathy. It is true that very little was known about the inward patternings of the novel during this period, but it was roundly condemned nonetheless.

Interpretation of *The Grapes of Wrath* became somewhat sounder in the period from 1954 to 1969, when critics began to examine its structure.[5] Although Northrop Frye pronounced, dismissively, that its "plot exists primarily to illustrate the [theme of] migratory labor . . . ,"[6] many in this period were discovering new perspectives. Particularly instructive in this connection was Warren French's analysis of the narrative. Answering an earlier criticism about the triviality and simplicity of the novel's plot (as if it represented a mere "Wagons West" romance), French showed that the novel was romantic in a more sophisticated way, embodying a version of the ancient quest motif: an exodus from a blighted land (Oklahoma) to a promised land (California).[7] This thesis spurred further work. Noting French's references to the Biblical flight from Egypt, other critics argued that Tom Joad and Jim Casy were in fact Biblical types, leaders in a journey out of exile, like Moses and Christ. Similarly, Rose of Sharon's milk, given to the starving man at the end of the novel, was seen to be a kind of manna ordained to sustain those not yet home from wandering, a gift of renewal to humankind. Such connections were elaborated gradually into complex systems of Biblical correlation and mythical interpretation. This second period of interpretation—wherein the number of books and articles grew rapidly—was marked generally by an increased willingness by readers to grant the book complexity. Few readers now were arguing that it was deeply flawed. In its first period a strictly social document, commonplace and oversimple, *The Grapes of Wrath* emerged during this second period as a fiction

---

[4]*On Native Grounds: An Interpretation of Modern American Prose Literature* (New York: Reynal and Hitchcock, 1942), pp. 394–397.

[5]"The Pattern of Criticism," pp. 701–704.

[6]*Anatomy of Criticism: Four Essays* (Princeton: Princeton University Press, 1957), p. 53.

[7]"Another Look at *The Grapes of Wrath*," *Colorado Quarterly*, 3 (Winter 1955): 337–343. This essay is collected in Warren French's *A Companion to "The Grapes of Wrath"* (Clifton, N.J.: A.M. Kelley, 1972).

richly connected to tradition and complex in its play of symbols and Biblical motifs.

Also given attention in this period were the novel's interchapters. These explicitly take a macrocosmic view of the Joads' dilemma and even, at times, propose and sort through solutions to social, economic, and spiritual problems. Since they also draw morals from segments of the action, they encourage the misconception that the novel is a complex, illustrated lesson—a didactic exercise presenting Steinbeck's ideas about human nature and social change. Initial readers complained of these chapters, but in 1958 Peter Lisca argued persuasively (in *The Wide World of John Steinbeck*) that they are not, in fact, wholly expository and that they provide important and often subtle connections between dramatic events. The interchapters, Lisca argues, guide the novel thematically in a way that actually intensifies the drama of the Joads' journey.[8] Subsequent readers—a little reluctantly, perhaps—have tended to agree with Lisca.

During this second wave of response, criticism turns from mere attack and defense to concentrate on fundamental issues of interpretation. Five of the twelve essays in this volume come from and exemplify the latter part of this second period. For example, in an extremely perceptive essay, George Bluestone discusses Edmund Wilson's view that the novel shows a "sentimental symbolism" and a "preoccupation with biology," arguing that it moves, in fact, in a very different direction—toward political radicalism and a truly sexual appreciation of nature (quite different from "biological" processes). In particular, Bluestone establishes that Tom Joad's status as a proletarian hero consists in part of a romantic tendency to merge an appreciation of the tillable earth with an appreciation of feminine "breasts, hips, [and] pelvis." Later assessments by J. Paul Hunter and R.W.B. Lewis on the effect of sentiment in the novel come to opposite conclusions. In its deployment of Biblical symbols, Hunter sees a genuine sense of "reaffirmation" and hope in an otherwise inhospitable modern world. Lewis, on the other hand, attributes to the intensity of its sentimental vein a destructive blurring of characterization—characters conceived not individually but as a corporate body—*en masse*. Another attempt to assess the book—by Edwin Bowden—finds it a traditional story of American isolation (people isolated from their community, and

[8](New Brunswick, N.J.: Rutgers University Press), pp. 156–160.

groups isolated from humanity), necessarily producing characters who are grotesques—misshapen and displaced types. The most formalistic study during this period is an essay by Robert J. Griffin and William A. Freedman treating Steinbeck's animal and mechanical imagery and showing how it helps to "bind together the Joad chapters with those [the interchapters] which generalize the meaning that the Joads' story illustrates." In this study Griffin and Freedman establish what has become a consensus reading of certain aspects of the novel.

As a group, these five essays clarify much that was earlier misunderstood. It is evident, for example, that the Joads move in an environment in which climatological, economic, and cultural forces have turned against them. The land has been depleted, the banks are mismanaged, and the people suffering from these misfortunes do not recognize their need to establish a "true" community. But as these five essays show, besides adversity in the Joads' world there is a natural receptivity to human purpose, even a sympathy for human designs. Conditions at present are unbearable, but these conditions are bringing about a spiritual and psychological change that, later, after more suffering, will be part of a new and better world. The narrative voice of the interchapters, as well as the narrative overall, testifies to the fact that, in spite of appearances to the contrary, suffering is meaningful, that the Joads' deep affinity with the natural world is impregnable, and that in time it will subdue the adversity of the moment. The family's unique power to "endure" derives from the same natural world that afflicts them. Thus, Steinbeck suggests repeatedly that adverse circumstances may be the agents of a "fortunate fall" and that after a period of desperate wandering and confusion, at a time projected into the ideal "future" the novel adumbrates, the wandering will end and the truly just community will exist. Implicit in every passage of the novel, in other words, particularly in the way Tom and Rose of Sharon are transformed in the novel's conclusion, is an apocalyptic promise. The Joads and people like them will rise and triumph.

George Bluestone's essay focuses on these highly romantic assumptions. He shows that there is a kind of unspoken collusion between human beings and nature. And in his discussion of the place of political radicalism in the book and in his interpretation of the "apotheosis of the . . . natural madonna" at the end of the novel, he establishes beyond doubt that this is a form of fiction wherein human purpose is reflected in, and cannot be separated from, the will of nature, a nature understood to be benevolent. In taking this view, the novel reflects what René Wellek calls the "great endeavor to overcome the split between subject and object, the self and the world"[9] and associates its vision unmistakably with that of romance—the nearest of all literary forms, as Northrop Frye explains, "to the wish-fulfillment dream."[10]

Reflections of nature's benevolence may be glimpsed also in other major episodes. In the famous chapter three, for example, a tortoise makes an unheroic trek across a highway and unwittingly helps an oat seed to make the same trip. The brief scene presents a succession of random acts, at the conclusion of which the oat seed is planted. En route to the planting, language and imagery draw a moral about a life force that can and will work through all available means. The novel stages a parallel drama in Jim Casy, who—like the tortoise—unwittingly carries a seed of thought and inspiration from Oklahoma to California. His Pelagian attitude toward human freedom germinates in California and becomes an intense belief in labor organization. When Jim Casy is killed, his belief takes root firmly in Tom Joad, who dedicates himself to union work. Tom's life becomes, in effect, the product of the impulse carried from Oklahoma. In short, despite adversity, a promise has been fulfilled.

At a higher level of abstraction, a romance of ideas is expressed vividly when specific material conditions in the Oklahoma dust bowl of the 1930s and in the Great Depression set in motion changes in the Joads' familial relations. Pa Joad is emasculated; the Joad grandparents, painfully uprooted, withdraw and die; Ma Joad reluctantly becomes head of the family. These changes occur as the Joads, pushed off their land, are forced to reexamine the relationship between human needs and the right of private ownership. As the disintegrating family moves closer to California, its remaining members, especially Ma Joad, are forced to acknowledge ties with the entire "human" community that replace the predominantly familial bonds of the old life in Oklahoma. These material developments, in turn, create the substance of Jim Casy's and Tom Joad's new awareness of social responsibility. At the end

---

[9]"Romanticism Re-Examined," in *Romanticism Reconsidered: Selected Papers from the English Institute,* Northrop Frye, ed. (New York: Columbia University Press, 1963), p. 132.

[10]*Anatomy of Criticism,* p. 186.

of this causal chain, Tom Joad—now awakened to economic needs—works to transform adverse conditions much like those that drove the Joads from Oklahoma in the first place. Here again, adversity is a disguised promise of benevolence that is on its way to fulfillment.

The same romantic tendency is expressed in what may seem an unlikely place. The novel elaborates specific ties between people and objects and expresses a definite attitude toward work. For example, on the Joads' trip to California their car breaks down—its engine has "blown" a "con-rod." In this elaborate sequence, after purchasing car parts in a wrecking yard, Tom Joad fixes the car with Al Joad's and Jim Casy's help. The reader is shown, at length, how oil must be drained, how the engine must be dismantled, and how piston rings must be fashioned from wire. Steinbeck's description of the final few steps shows an almost obsessional concern with accurate details:

> Casy knelt down and took the flashlight. He kept the beam on the working hands as they patted the gasket gently in place and lined the holes with the pan bolts. The two men strained at the weight of the pan, caught the end bolts, and then set in the others; and when they were all engaged, Tom took them up little by little until the pan settled evenly in against the gasket, and he tightened hard against the nuts.
>
> "I guess that's her," Tom said. He tightened the oil tap, looked carefully up at the pan, and took the light and searched the ground. "There she is. Let's get the oil back in her."
>
> They crawled out and poured the bucket of oil back in the crank case. Tom inspected the gasket for leaks.
>
> "O.K., Al. Turn her over," he said.

The emphasis of the scene, as of most of the passage, falls on the characteristics of car parts and on the "true" process of fixing the engine—exactly as both might be described in nonfictional prose. Yet the apparent realism is in fact highly specialized, for implicit in the structure of the scene is an insistence that "objects" may signify a predetermined human purpose. Careful elaboration of the repair process directs the reader to affirm that a connecting rod means a connecting rod, a functioning part of an engine. A wrench means only a wrench, and so on. That is, the clarity of this scene is produced by a one-to-one correspondence of "con-rod" (as signifier) and its purely functional meaning (as signified). The exclusive meaning of the scene, furthermore, is that the disabled car gets fixed by the three men.

The function of such "objects" in other early twentieth-century novels indicates by contrast how truly unusual Steinbeck's "object" realism is. In Theodore Dreiser's *Sister Carrie* (1900), for instance, universally pronounced a highly realistic novel, objects bristle with economic, social, and moral significance. Carrie's clothes, the rocking chair she sits in, the buildings she walks around, the machines she works at—all speak articulately of Carrie and her social and economic world. Objects in Dreiser—never mere things—have indeterminate social and economic implications. Likewise, in Henry James's *The Ambassadors* (1903), objects become mysterious hieroglyphs: each balustrade, Parisian street, and landscape implies something about human relationships and may be read and interpreted in that light. In Edith Wharton's *The Age of Innocence* (1920), even the fold of a dress, the position of a platform on a beach, the facade of an apartment—all serve to indicate social placement. In virtually any sampling of American novels before 1939, physical objects signify the presence of complex fictional relationships.

Steinbeck's car repair scene, on the other hand, like many other work scenes in *The Grapes of Wrath,* locks physical objects in a single position. The connecting rod does *not* signify a plurality of possible associations, and the dark crankcase oil has no associations at all except as engine lubricant. Associations different from these are abruptly foreclosed by the unusual militancy of the car repair process. Rather, the scene presents objects as nonfunctioning signifiers, broken meanings that assert a neutral resistance, one to be overcome and defined by the three men. By thus depicting objects so that they approximate a semblance of dull matter, with only their immediate use and function to define them, the scene presents a strictly mimetic vision of work as the transformation of material into usable goods. Objects in the scene create the neutral resistance of undone work, and the one-dimensional presentation of the scene shows men *bringing* meaning to the objects they touch, objects that speak only of clearly articulated human ends. By restricting the associations of physical objects in this way, Steinbeck creates a linguistic guarantee that work has a predetermined meaning and is a humanly purposeful activity; for in this scene human desire is projected in the relations of people and objects as clearly as the human form of "breasts, hips, [and] pelvis" is etched in the earth beneath Tom Joad's feet. This depiction of human desire and of its sympathetic reception in the material world leads back along a circuitous route to what Northrop Frye shows to be the substance of a "wish-fulfillment dream"—an environment separate from human beings but receptive to their desires. Here work is the mysterious link between human beings and the environment, and the channel through which human desire is guaranteed a home in the world. The romance of work, as Steinbeck abundantly demonstrates, is reflected not only in the car repair scene but also in the grand scheme of the Joads' quest. Their work, the novel promises, will pay off.

The other seven essays in this collection come from a third period of response to *The Grapes of Wrath*: 1971 to 1982. These, like most current criticism, analyze the book as a development of the epic and romance traditions. Like J. Paul Hunter earlier, Leonard Lutwack emphasizes the theme of "affirmation," which he relates to the heroic affirmation of the *Aeneid*. "Of all Steinbeck's heroes," he remarks, "[Tom Joad] is the only one who affirms the possibility of a hero arising out of the anonymity of twentieth-century economic strife and still bearing the signs of an ancient dedication." Warren French and Peter Lisca, in new essays of this period, reaffirm Lutwack's view, anticipated indeed in their own earlier studies, which trace in the novel the struggles of a benevolent life force to endure and triumph. Also in this period Mary Ellen Caldwell elaborates Lisca's work on the effectiveness of the interchapters.

The other three studies from this last period are less sympathetic. Horst Groene sees a reconciliation in the novel of industrial and agrarian forces that makes many of the conflicts in which the Joads traditionally are thought to be suffering unreal, or at least less pressing for their community. Through Al Joad (Groene believes), increasingly an independent and attractive figure, Steinbeck has depicted the opening of a new "frontier of opportunity" in California (the promised land) and, in effect, drained away some of the effect of the novel's otherwise melancholy ending. Stuart L. Burns goes further and directly questions the legitimacy of the novel's ending; he claims that a thin veneer of affirmation conceals "a logical and inexorable movement toward tragedy or pathos." The novel's ending in this view exemplifies

American culture's traditional inability to reconcile the self-reliant person with the needs and wishes of society. The vision of apparent reconciliation in the novel's conclusion, Burns asserts, is an inappropriate and dishonest effect of melodrama.

One last area of romance, little discussed in criticism so far, is specifically sexual. For example, in the novel's last scene Rose of Sharon turns her young body into a cradle for an old man and appears to be serving the *human* (not specifically familial) community to which Tom Joad is newly dedicated. In this pose she embodies the vitalism characteristic of Steinbeck's sensibility throughout the novel and becomes a kind of nature spirit, a goddess. The following paragraph, the last of the novel, shows her apotheosis into a figure of transcendence:

> For a minute Rose of Sharon sat still in the whispering barn. Then she hoisted her tired body up and drew the comfort about her. She moved slowly to the corner and stood looking down at the wasted face, into the wide, frightened eyes. Then slowly she lay down beside him. He shook his head slowly from side to side. Rose of Sharon loosened one side of the blanket and bared her breast. "You got to," she said. She squirmed closer and pulled his head close. "There!" she said. "There." Her hand moved behind his head and supported it. Her fingers moved gently in his hair. She looked up and across the barn, and her lips came together and smiled mysteriously.

Central here—crystallized in the Mona Lisa smile—is the assertion in a highly romantic episode of the same idealized nature spirit as is present in Steinbeck's Salinas sagas and in the whole of his fictional world. Institutions—whether the Oklahoma banks or the California unions—may falter (institutions do falter, and Tom Joad may fail). But human desire, transcending all barriers, cannot fail in this world. This last scene epitomizes the novelist's faith in romantic sentiment, out of which comes all familial and social change, all political organization, all human activity. The historical dialectic may or may not operate; unions may or may not change the quality of life; but the mysterious vitalism of Rose of Sharon remains indestructible.

Yet important as women are in *The Grapes of Wrath,* the serious work of social revolution—especially that which Tom Joad undertakes—is *man*'s work. Rose of Sharon and Ma Joad make possible survival and growth, but it is the men finally who must build the new community. Tom Joad draws his inspiration from Ma Joad but then goes forth "as a man" to remake the world. At the end of the novel, he, not she, is transformed into a spirit of the labor movement (like Joe Hill), a kind of Pan who will be everywhere simultaneously to comfort and to aid all working people in their struggle to organize. Joan Hedrick (in the newest essay in this collection) examines the ideological implications of this romantic sexual mythology, drawing attention to a special intensity in the novel's mother-son relationship. Hedrick sees the quasi-incestuous tie between Tom and Ma Joad as a model of the male-female as well as political relations in the novel. Ultimately, she maintains, the novel confirms rather than undercuts the bourgeois myths that support certain sexual relations. Further, the depiction of Tom Joad as a celibate son-lover suggests a deep rejection of the familial concept, a rejection more complex and emphatic than previous readers have seen. Hedrick's insights in this area are useful, the more so because criticism has so far yielded no other significant analysis of female roles either in this novel or in Steinbeck's other work.

We have been slow to read this novel well, perhaps because on the surface at least—as is true of much popular, romantic fiction— it appears to offer few problems. The evocation of and quarrel with the past that distinguishes many twentieth-century novels are little evident in *The Grapes of Wrath*. Its form is not highly innovative by modernist standards, and it does not demand particular erudition of its readers. Rather, in open defiance of the mainstream of twentieth-century literature, it establishes its own unique ties to the Anglo-American tradition, and in this role—along with much fiction by Robert Penn Warren, William Styron, Saul Bellow, Chaim Potok, and others—makes part of a continuing romantic tradition, one strongly tied to the Gothic and popular romances of the nineteenth century.

PART ONE
Interpretations

The Commonplace
and the Grotesque

by Edwin T. Bowden

John Steinbeck's *The Grapes of Wrath* marked another step for
the modern age when it took up the question of isolation not only
for a few particular characters but for a whole people, and considered it in a novel that belongs in many respects with *The Rise of
Silas Lapham* and *Winesburg, Ohio* in a group of the grotesque and
the commonplace. It is a novel of the agricultural depression of
the 1930's and that memory of the folly and failure of man, the
dust bowl. Yet it is a novel not about conditions but about people,
the commonplace people of a Howells—even though Howells
would have been shocked at the novel itself. Steinbeck's despair
and indignation are too great for a Howells, and his characters are
far from the familiar society of a Howells. Like Anderson and
Faulkner, in contrast to Howells, he even questions the assumption of free will in the individual. Yet his people must meet the
commonplace problems of life—food, shelter, clothing, medical
aid—and their desires are the desires of the commonplace man—
happiness, love, family unity, self-respect, a feeling of belonging.
They are the common men of the new century. In another sense,
however, the novel is not about commonplace man but about a
special, often grotesque group of men, the Okies, the dispossessed
of the dust bowl, the new itinerant farm laborers of California.
And one of the successes of the novel is the manner in which it
conveys simultaneously the impression, almost an epic impression, of a whole people migrating westward and the familiar view
of one particular family facing its particular problems. The Joad

family, even though unique, is a part of a whole people; and this novel, unlike most of the novels of the previous century, is as much about a people as it is about a few central people. In the midst of a blighting depression the concern for the individual begins to give way to the concern for the people, even though paradoxically it was this novel, probably more than any other, that convinced America that the group scornfully called Okies was after all made up of familiar and commonplace individuals.

There are isolated and lonely and even grotesque individuals in the novel. Uncle John, the "lonest goddamn man in the world," [94][1] who let his wife die of appendicitis, thinking it only a stomach ache, is forever after lost in his sense of guilt, a marked and isolated man in his own mind. Casy, the former preacher who has lost his old faith, is a lonely man looking for some new faith. And Muley Graves, who stays behind in Oklahoma, is only a lonely ghost haunting an empty land:

> "I'd tell myself, 'I'm lookin' after things so when all the folks come back it'll be all right.' But I knowed that wan't true. There ain't nothin' to look after. The folks ain't never comin' back. I'm jus' wanderin' aroun' like a damn ol' graveyard ghos'." [69]

But Casy and Muley are parts of a larger pattern, the isolation of a people. Casy is to be their spokesman, finally to give words to their deepest feeling, and Muley is a result of the people's migration and a sign of their departure. For the central isolation of the novel is that of a whole people. Driven from home and land, they have lost the sense of belonging: " 'Place where folks live is them folks. They ain't whole, out lonely on the road in a piled-up car. They ain't alive no more.' " [71] At home they had been a part of the land, had belonged to it and had felt their roots go down. Then came the drought and the banks and the tractors, and suddenly there was a home no longer, there was no place to belong to. And without a country there is only lonely wandering. The young and the strong can bear the isolation, but for the old, too long rooted, it is like leaving life itself. Grampa dies before they can even carry him out of the state.

The people have lost their old home and cannot find a new one. No one somewhere else wants them to belong; no one wants them

---

[1]Page references are to John Steinbeck, *The Grapes of Wrath* (New York: The Viking Press, 1939).

at all. On the migration west, California shines ahead as a newer and greener home. But along the way, prophetically, they are met only with hatred and suspicion and contempt, tempered occasionally with a touch of human pity. California does not even have the pity. On first arrival at the California line a fellow Okie had offered the Joads a warning not believed then but soon to prove too true:

> "People gonna have a look in their eye. They gonna look at you an' their face says, 'I don't like you, you son-of-a-bitch.' Gonna be deputy sheriffs, an' they'll push you aroun'. You camp on the roadside, an' they'll move you on. You gonna see in people's face how they hate you." [280]

There the people are scared for fear their country in turn will be taken from them by this new horde of hungry and landless and homeless, and they try to drive them away by fair means or foul. The Californians are willing to use them for gain, to demand the greatest work for the least pay, knowing the hungry cannot refuse, but never to offer them permanence or a home, never a country of their own. The Joads and their kind, the new migratory people are as isolated from this country as from their own far behind, unable to live there, unwanted here. If they settle for a moment, they are soon driven off by hunger or by pick handles. And if they complain or protest, they are reds or agitators or dangerous vagrants, and the police and the mobs are eager for violence. There is no immediate solution—whatever history with its slow movement may later have provided—and the lonely people seem destined to wander forever in isolation. It is fitting that the novel ends with the Joads wiser and more experienced, but still with no sense of belonging, no permanence in the country, no home of their own.

With no sense of belonging to anything outside, the people must turn within their own group for comfort and strength and loss of loneliness. The family is the all-important unit, as it was in *My Antonia,* as it must be when there is nothing else to which to belong with any meaning. Before the migration the Joad family had been scattered about their region, but it comes together for the great trek, and its unity is a large part of its strength. Ma, at the center of the family, soon becomes the accepted leader and the source of unity and confidence and will; and her one unvarying demand is for the family to stay together no matter what happens: " 'All we got is the family unbroke. Like a bunch a cows, when the lobos are ranging, stick all together. I ain't scared while we're all here, all that's alive, but I ain't gonna see us bust up.' " [231] And she is right. Like the Lapham family, although so different in surface and in circumstance, as long as the family is together there is no isolation for the individual member, whatever his weakness and his failure. Ma can be fierce in her determination, and she can even back up her demands with a jack handle when necessary, for she knows that the family is all that they have left to depend upon: " 'What we got lef' in the worl'? Nothin' but us. Nothin' but the folks.' " [230] But despite her wisdom and her determination the family unity does begin to crumble, and it is the nearest to a real defeat that the Joads ever reach. Grampa and Granma die along the way, Noah leaves the family at the California border, Connie abandons Rosasharn and the family, Tom is driven away by the sheriffs and by his conscience, and at the end of the story Al is about to leave with his new promised wife. Some of these losses are inevitable and unavoidable, others are the result of too great an individual weakness, but each tends to lessen the fierce family loyalty and will that carry the Joads through their trials and their loneliness. If the Joads are ever broken—and even in their reduced numbers it is hard to imagine—it will be because the family itself is broken. But affairs never reach that desperate a state and never will as long as Ma is there to hold the rest of the family together in defiance of the hostile world.

An awareness of the value and the comfort of the family is not limited to the Joads, of course, but is an element of the entire migration. And under the pressures of a common need the whole people slowly become one large family in themselves. The Joads, the particular example, find themselves losing a few members of the real family but quickly picking up others who are accepted almost as real members. The family in the long run does not diminish but rather expands more and more. Preacher Casy had early been accepted as a member, and along the road Mr. and Mrs. Wilson are added until sickness forces them out again. Others move more quickly in and out. But these are simply examples of a continuous process in which all the people find themselves increasingly drawn into a larger family relationship. Camping along Route 66 headed west, the process begins: "In the evening a strange thing happened: the twenty families became one family, the children were the children of all. The loss of home

became one loss, and the golden time in the West was one dream."
[264]

In the West itself in the face of united hostility the process is
even stronger, as it must be. Soon the world for the Joads is
divided into "our kind of folks" or even just "our folks" and the
hostile "them." And here the larger family must stand together if it
is to stand at all, and the lesser family, the literal family, is just the
starting point. Even Ma recognizes the new fact as she thanks the
woman who had shared their temporary housing in a boxcar and
helped with Rosasharn's delivery:

> "You been frien'ly," she said. "We thank you."
> The stout woman smiled. "No need to thank. Ever'body's in the
> same wagon. S'pose we was down. You'd a give us a han'."
> "Yes," Ma said, "we would."
> "Or anybody."
> "Or anybody. Use' ta be the fambly was fust. It ain't so now. It's
> anybody. Worse off we get, the more we got to do." [606]

Among the Okies struggling to exist in an alien land the family of
man is more than a sentimental phrase. It is a practical and a
necessary fact of existence.

The family of man is more even than a necessity for the Joads: it
is an ideal of the novel. At the lowest level it appears in a form
familiar during the depression, the hopeful ideal of men working
together in some form of unity to protect their economic and
social rights. Only organized resistance of many can demand a fair
wage, for instance, and the idea is illustrated in the strike led by
Preacher Casy against the peach growers. When he is killed for his
efforts he is a martyr to a worthy ideal, although most of the
people do not even recognize the fact. Or when the migrants band
together to run the camp at Weedpatch, a camp that is clean,
decent, orderly, and without deputy sheriffs from outside, the
people are beginning to move toward a social ideal. These are
ideals that present themselves immediately to the people, for they
are caught in a life-or-death struggle in which money and living
conditions are of vital concern, and on the surface at least are the
only concerns. But in the novel as a whole they are simply
corollaries of a greater concern with the ideal of the family of man,
of the moving, as Steinbeck puts it, from "I" to "we." [206] Here
Preacher Casy is the spokesman for the ideal, stating it directly,

and the one who attempts as well to live it, although he ends by dying for it.

When Casy first appears in the novel he is a troubled man who has lost his first sure faith, but, unlike the Reverend Gail Hightower, he has never lost the spirit of a faith or the sure desire of a faith. He is a lost and lonely man wandering in the wilderness to question his own mind and to define just what it is that he does believe. But whatever his doubts, he knows he still has a mission to perform: " 'Here I got the sperit sometimes an' nothin' to preach about. I got the call to lead people, an' no place to lead 'em.' " [29] In the trek to California he finds a place to lead the people, and along the way he finds a faith to preach. The faith is a love of people themselves and a belief in a total soul of humanity and is participated in by all men, a commonality of man in the sight of God that makes one man alone an incomplete creature: " 'not one fella for another fella, but one fella kind of harnessed to the whole shebang—that's right, that's holy.' " [110] Then when his half-understood philosophy is brought up against the injustice of the world his way ahead is clear. His first chance to put his belief into dramatic action comes when he offers himself to save Tom and a friend from a bullying sheriff. His second comes when he leads the strike against starvation pay in the peach orchard. There he is killed by the representatives of a harsher and a more selfish law. But his preaching will go on through the lips of Tom Joad, who has inherited his belief and, thinking back to Casy's words, can say, " 'But I know now a fella ain't no good alone.' " [570] There is the central point of the novel, and there is the conviction on which the overt social protest of the novel is based.

Casy believes that his new faith is not Christianity, even though he finds texts in *Ecclesiastes* to make his point. Perhaps it is not, although in effect it reaches the same belief in the brotherhood of man under the fatherhood of God. Certainly it is not the hell-fire, damnation, washed-in-the-blood, shout-to-the-Lamb religion that Casy and most of his flock had known before. It is perhaps nearer to a moral humanism with the Christian tradition behind it. But whatever it is, it teaches that a man cannot live by and for himself alone. When early in the novel Tom Joad says, " 'I'm just tryin' to get along without shovin' nobody around,' " [13–14] he suggests, too, another paradoxical aspect of the same thought. For the novel seems divided into those who are intent on hurting others and

those who want to avoid hurting others. The moral assumption is
that a man must lead his own life as best he can, and others must
allow him to if possible: " 'On'y one thing in this worl' I'm sure of,
an' that's I'm sure nobody got a right to mess with a fella's life. He
got to do it all hisself. Help him, maybe, but not tell him what to
do.' " [306] The only demand is that his life must not hurt others.
The common belief lying behind both assumptions, the need for a
feeling of the mutual ties of humanity and the need for allowing a
man to lead his life unmolested, is the belief in the value of the
individual life. And both the cause and the result of this belief are
the ideal of love of humanity or the human spirit. Casy, in hesi-
tantly defining his beliefs, must inevitably work through the point:
" 'Maybe . . . it's all men an' all women we love; maybe that's the
Holy Sperit—the human sperit—the whole shebang.' " [32–33]
The life of all humanity is holy, and so must be the life of the
individual within it. With the love of others, the love of humanity
given and taken, loneliness is impossible, even in the midst of
isolation. The trouble is that not all men are so morally committed, and those who are must often suffer isolation from the
others.

   In *The Grapes of Wrath* there are plenty of "others" to hold the
Okies in isolation. Sometimes they act out of the brutality and
hatred born of fear, as the deputies who destroy the Hooverville
camps. Sometimes they act out of selfishness and desire for
personal gain, as the orchard owners who break up the strike
against starvation wages. But whatever the immediate motivation,
all deny the humanity and the individual worth of the Okies. The
service-station boy on Route 66, even though he takes no direct
action, is representative in his thought:

> "Well, you and me got sense. Them goddamn Okies got no sense
> and no feeling. They ain't human. A human being wouldn't live
> like they do. A human being couldn't stand it to be so dirty and
> miserable. They ain't a hell of a lot better than gorillas." [301]

Against the isolation imposed by such an attitude the Okies see no
recourse beyond banding together more solidly in mutual aid and
understanding. If at times they believe too much in mere organization for its own sake—defended in part by the assumption of the
common nature of man—their longing can be understood in
terms of the times and their situation. The "others," after all, have

banded together, not out of a desire to serve their common humanity, but rather out of a selfish desire to exploit the unorganized. For the individual to fight back alone may be heroic, but it is fatal. As an extreme case of the isolated individual against the world the story of Pretty Boy Floyd is mentioned again and again: " 'They run him like a coyote, an' him a-snappin' an' a-snarlin', mean as a lobo.' " [103] But the Okies of this novel do not turn into that sort of outlaw. Driven out of the home and the society they once knew, wandering in isolation among those who cannot even accept them as members of a common humanity, they can only turn to each other for help and understanding and love. And there, bound together by their mutual plight, forced into a recognition of the humanity of others, they can lose the loneliness that their isolation threatens.

For all its modern setting, then, for all its time of unusual conditions and its interest in a whole people as well as in the individual, *The Grapes of Wrath* is still clearly in the tradition of the American concern in fiction for the problem of isolation. It has simply broadened the theme, in keeping with the sociological interest imposed by the century, to include a group rather than a single person. The Joads must each meet the problem of alienation in his own way, yet behind the individual there is always the family, and behind the family there is always the whole tribe of migrants, each individual and each group of which must meet the problem too. And the answer for all is still the old answer for the individual: the loss of self in concern and love for others. If man can lose his exclusively egocentric and selfish interest to turn outward to others, he need not fear loneliness or spiritual isolation. For this century the mechanics of the solution may be somewhat different from those of earlier days. Man can no longer simply turn to humanity—desirable as that ideal is—but must belong to some form of group to which to turn. Even then the answer is not simple, for the group may itself be devoted to inhumane ends, as is the organization of farmers and canners in this novel. So man must turn to the group, and the group must turn to humanity itself. The individual is no longer in complete control of his own end, as Anderson and Faulkner imply, but must depend upon others as well as himself. But the others, as *The Grapes of Wrath* insists so successfully, are themselves individuals. And if the individuals of this modern complex, organized world would always keep faith with their common humanity in their necessary organization, the ideal world in which there is no isolation and no loneliness would be achieved. The goal may never be reached— and the fiction of this century is hardly optimistic—but man in the meanwhile has an immediate answer that will serve his needs and will eventually help the step toward the ideal. When man can turn out of himself to others he can escape spiritual loneliness, whatever his isolation may be.

With *The Grapes of Wrath* one method of presenting the theme of isolation reaches fulfillment, if not climax, making way undoubtedly for other methods to be slowly developed. When William Dean Howells began insisting that the novel must be realistic in presenting the commonplace of American life, he probably never imagined that realism would include the grotesque as well—in fact he would probably have said that the two are contradictory—or that the commonplace in a new age would be a matter of a whole people in despair as well as of a few individuals concerned with the decencies of daily life. Yet that is what happened, though literary historians may want to trace the development along other and equally satisfactory paths. The theme of isolation, however, remained a constant, even though the method of presenting it and the fictional situations in which it was dramatized varied as American life varied to meet the new needs. And the majority of novelists considering that new American life agreed that the old and traditional answer to isolation, however difficult or impossible it might be to attain, remained not only valid but still the only valid answer. It had to answer new demands of the warped and psychologically wounded, it had to meet new doubts of the final free will of man, it even had to apply to a whole helpless sociological group as well as to the strong and independent individual, but it still met the demand. If some novels were doubtful or skeptical, it was not so much of the answer as of the possibility of accepting and living with that answer. Isolation in the new America, it seemed, was not really so different after all from isolation in the old. The theme and its conclusion were too basic and too traditional in American life to alter even in the new and changing novel.

From Naturalism to the Drama of Consciousness—The Education of the Heart in *The Grapes of Wrath*

by Warren French

Apparently the novel that was to become *The Grapes of Wrath* (1939) was written originally in the same bitterly ironic, pessimistic vein as *In Dubious Battle* and *Of Mice and Men*. In a letter to his agents and publishers in June, 1938, Steinbeck announced the decision that marked the most significant turning point in his career as an artist. He called a sixty-five thousand word novel, which was tentatively entitled "L'Affaire Lettuceberg," a "bad book"—what his father would have called a "smart-alec book"—and announced that it could not be published. "My whole work drive has been aimed at making people understand each other," he continued; "and then I deliberately write this book, the aim of which is to cause hatred through partial understanding."[1]

Steinbeck pushed himself to finish a new version by autumn; and the result was *The Grapes of Wrath*, a novel that begins—with its description of a land devastated by dust storms and the slow, determined plodding of a land turtle—like the Naturalistic works that Steinbeck had been writing for nearly a decade. However, the narrative becomes something quite different—a story of the awakening of man's consciousness that coincides with the awakening of his conscience. This change is signaled in the fourteenth chapter by an interpolated credo about the uniqueness of man: "This you may say of man—when theories change and crash, when schools, philosophies, when narrow dark alleys of thought, national,

"From Naturalism to the Drama of Consciousness." From *John Steinbeck* by Warren French (Boston: Twayne Publishers, Inc., a division of G. K. Hall & Co., 1975), pp. 92–102. Revised edition, copyright 1975 by Twayne Publishers, Inc. Reprinted by permission of the publisher.
[1]Lisca, *The Wide World of John Steinbeck* (New Brunswick, N.J., 1958), p. 147.

religious, economic, grow and disintegrate, man reaches, stumbles forward, painfully, mistakenly sometimes. Having stepped forward, he may slip back, but only half a step, never the full step back" (204–05).[2] This credo underlies Steinbeck's fiction for the rest of his life, and it is given its final form in his pronouncement during his Nobel Prize acceptance speech: "I hold that a writer who does not passionately believe in the perfectibility of man has no dedication nor any membership in literature."

The writer of *In Dubious Battle* and *Of Mice and Men* gives no evidence of believing in the perfectibility of man; the writer who rewrote "L'Affaire Lettuceberg" into *The Grapes of Wrath* does. The central story of the big novel is of the Joad family's taking the step forward that Steinbeck describes in the fourteenth chapter. This novel is not a *static* one about long-suffering Jobs; it is a *dynamic* one about people who learn that survival depends upon their adapting to new conditions. This point—that the novel tells a dynamic story about learning to change—has often, however, been missed, as is illustrated by widespread misconceptions about the tableau that unmistakably ends the story that Steinbeck has chosen to tell, even though it presents no lasting solution to the real-life situation of the migrant workers who inspired the fiction.

In the final chapter, Ma Joad leads the remnants of her "fambly" from their flood-engulfed boxcar to a dry barn on high land. There Rosasharn, whose baby has been stillborn, feeds from her breast an old man on the point of death who cannot be nourished otherwise. Although it would seem that only the prurient, who have missed the point that the plight of these people is desperate, could object to this poignant scene, it has been a bone of contention since the novel appeared. Among the early reviewers, Clifton Fadiman wrote in the *New Yorker,* that "the ending is the tawdriest kind of fake symbolism." Later, French critic Claude-Edmond Magny argued that the novel ends on "a purely poetic image which in no way brings the plot to a conclusion." Even such a standard reference work as James Hart's *Oxford Companion to American Literature* maintains the position that Steinbeck fails to complete his story, "the value of whose conclusion is purely symbolic." Thus it is charged either that the conclusion concludes nothing or that it is not prepared for by any overall

[2]Page references are to *"The Grapes of Wrath": Text and Criticism,* edited by Peter Lisca (New York, 1972).

allegorical structure. My thesis is that both charges are wrong and that the Joad story in *The Grapes of Wrath* is—like *The Red Pony*—a consistent allegory that is concluded logically and fittingly by Rosasharn's gesture and that, furthermore—as the author himself suggests—a reader may find "five layers" in the book.[3]

In a sociological sense, of course, the novel is unfinished because Steinbeck does not tell us whether the migrants survive or disappear. At the time he wrote, he didn't know what the outcome of their struggles would be. He implied, however, that the actions of the reader might have a bearing on the situation, just as a great predecessor had in a novel that is in many ways similar and that certainly might have lent its title to Steinbeck's. At the end of *Hard Times*, Charles Dickens directly addresses his "Dear reader": "it rests with you and me, whether, in our two fields of action, similar things shall be or not. Let them be!" As for the solution of the real problems that the novels reflect, Dickens and Steinbeck leave it to the readers in their "field of action"—the real world; the novelist's field of action is literary allegory, not sociological prophecy.

I

The Education of the Heart

The story of the Joads, insofar as it concerns the novelist, is completed in the barn; for the novel is not about the family's quest for security but about their education, which is shown to be completed in the final scene.

What "education"?—the education of the heart, the same kind of education that Thomas Gradgrind receives painfully in *Hard Times* and that provides the principal link between these two powerful and controversial works. In *The Grapes of Wrath*, this education results in a change from the family's jealously regarding itself as an isolated and self-important clan to its envisioning itself as part of one vast human family that, in preacher Casy's words, shares "one big soul ever'body's a part of" (33). The novel is not so much concerned with the frustrating physical migration

---

[3]Lisca reprints in the edition cited in footnote 2 (pp. 858–59), a letter from Steinbeck to Pascal Covici, written early in 1939, in which Steinbeck defends the ending of the novel and observes that a reader will find as many "layers" as he can and "won't find more than he has in himself."

described—much as Steinbeck's unsparing picture of contemporary conditions may have accounted for the phenomenal reception of the novel—as with the accompanying spiritual movement that is akin to the one celebrated in Walt Whitman's "Passage to India."

Casy, the former preacher, has already meditated upon the idea of a brotherhood of all men before the story begins, but he cannot formulate clearly his concept. He finds it difficult to explain his idea that "maybe it's all men an' all women we love" (32) because "fella gets use' to a way of thinkin', it's hard to leave" (69). When he finds confirmation of his theory in Muley Graves's observation, "If a fella's got somepin to eat an' another fella's hungry—why, the first fella ain' got no choice," Casy feels obliged to say, "Muley's got a-holt of somepin, an' it's too big for him, an' it's too big for me" (66). The difficulty of clarifying his new idea had become evident when he and Tom Joad had reached the deserted Joad house and Casy had confessed, "If I was still a preacher I'd say the arm of the Lord has struck. But now I don't know what's happened" (55). Still, he is able to exemplify his new ideas when he replies to Ma Joad's objection that cutting pork is women's work, "It's all work. . . . They's too much of it to split up to men's or women's work" (146).

When Casy finally figures out in a California jail what he does believe, he explains his ideas in the form of a parable that illustrates the benefits of unified action. Speaking of the inmates, he says,

> "Well, they was nice fellas, ya see. What made 'em bad was they needed stuff. An' I begin to see, then. It's need that makes all the trouble. I ain't got it worked out. Well, one day they give us some beans that was sour. One fella started yellin', an' nothin' happened. He yelled his head off. Trusty come along an' looked in an' went on. Then another fella yelled. Well, sir, then we all got yellin'. And we all got on the same tone. . . . Then somepin happened! They come a-runnin', and they give us some other stuff to eat—give it to us. Ya see?" (521–22).

At the moment, Tom Joad doesn't see; and Casy observes, "Maybe I can't tell you. . . . Maybe you got to find out" (522). The novel depicts the Joads' "finding out."

They are a difficult case, for *The Grapes of Wrath* is not a tale of the conversion of the easily susceptible. The family's haughty, isolated attitude at the beginning of the novel is illustrated by Tom's remark to a friendly truckdriver: "Nothin' ain't none of your affair except skinnin' this here bull-bitch along, an' that's the least thing you work at" (18). Tom is not a thinker. When Casy tells him, "They's gonna come a thing that's gonna change the whole country," Tom simply replies, "I'm still layin' my dogs down one at a time" (237). Uncle John, who has been responsible for his wife's death, comes closest to understanding that something exists that is beyond the family, but he attributes the failures that result from his selfishness to "sin," and he indulges in disorganized acts of charity that lead Pa Joad to comment that he "give away about ever'thing he got, an' still he ain't very happy" (92).

Ma, whom Steinbeck calls "the citadel of the family" (100), views the trip to California only in terms of the family's success. She ponders, "I wonder—that is, if we all get jobs an' all work— maybe we can get one of them little white houses" (124). Although she burns her souvenirs to sever herself from the past (148), she does so because she thinks primarily of her importance to the family. When Tom asks if she's not "scared" that the new place won't be "nice like we thought," she replies, "No, I ain't. . . . Up ahead they's a thousan' lives we might live, but when it comes, it'll on'y be one. . . . it's jus' the road goin' by for me. . . . All the rest'd get upset if I done any more'n that. They all depen' on me jus' thinkin' about that" (168–69).

When Ma threatens Pa with a jack-handle to prevent the family's splitting up, she argues, "All we got is the family unbroke. Like a bunch of cows, when the lobos are ranging, stick all together. I ain't scared while we're all here, all that's alive, but I ain't gonna see us bust up" (231). She still seeks rationalizations that will incorporate the Wilsons into the family rather than make assistance to them appear to be help to strangers. "We got almost a kin bond," she tells Sairy; "Grampa, he died in your tent" (227). And she insists that Casy not write the note to be pinned to Grampa's body because the preacher "wan't no kin" (195).

But the family disintegrates in spite of Ma's brave efforts and her bold protests. The dog is killed on the highway. Grampa dies of a stroke before the family crosses the Oklahoma border, and Granma dies before they have reached the fertile valleys of California. Because each death symbolizes an inability to adjust to the changed conditions imposed by the migration, it does not challenge the family's basic unity. Ma is more severely shaken by the departure of the oldest son Noah to live "beside a nice river" (284), and she is forced to observe, "Family's fallin' apart. . . . I don' know. Seems like I can't think no more" (294). Most alarming, however, is the disappearance of Rose of Sharon's husband Connie Rivers because his running away shatters a potential family unit that is just in the process of forming.

Ma's family pride is shattered in other ways. She is disturbed by the California border patrolman from whom she first hears the term "Okie" when he tells her, "We don't want none of you settlin' down here" (291). Then she is upset by the vigilance committee which warns the family, "We ain't gonna have no goddam Okies in this town" (382). Despite these affronts and her insistence on sharing with the Wilsons over their protests, she still thinks primarily in terms of the family unit. Her reaction upon arriving in Bakersfield is "the fambly's here" (311), and in the encounter with the vigilantes she counsels Tom to do nothing because "the fambly's breakin' up" (381).

The first significant change in the family's attitude occurs in the Weedpatch government camp where the Wallaces share their work with Tom, although they may thereby cut their own meager earnings. The self-governing arrangement of the camp also makes the Joads feel like decent people again. Evaluating her recent experiences, Ma says, ". . . in Needles, that police. He done somepin to me, made me feel mean. Made me feel ashamed. An' now I ain't ashamed. These folks is our folks. . . . Why, I feel like people again" (420); but she prefaces her remarks with the reminder, "We're Joads," and she still talks about settling the family in a little white cottage. At this camp the Joads meet people who do not think of cooperation as "charity," but all is not harmonious even here. A religious bigot attacks Rose of Sharon, and the women of the camp stage a garbage fight. Pa Joad is still far from won over to Casy's way of thinking—"I can't starve so's you can get two bits," he tells another man in a quarrel about taking others' jobs for lower wages (463).

The easy atmosphere of the government camp, where—as one man observes—"We're all a-workin' together" (488), is in striking contrast to the tense atmosphere at the Hooper Ranch. There the prevailing attitudes are epitomized by a checker's remark that putting holes in the bottom of buckets "keeps people from stealing them" (506). Here Ma learns "one thing good"—"If you're in trouble or hurt or need—go to poor people. They're the only ones that'll help—the only ones" (513–14). The Joads still think of help, however, only as a means towards maintaining the family. When Casy, now a labor organizer, pleads with Tom to support a strike against the ranch, Tom replies, "Pa wouldn' do it. . . . He'd say it wasn't none of his business. . . . Think Pa's gonna give up his meat on account a other fellas?" (524).

A family crisis is precipitated at the ranch by Tom's impetuously killing the man who has killed Casy. Tom decides that he must run away because, as he tells Ma, he "can't go puttin' this on you folks." Ma retorts angrily, ". . . goin' away ain't gonna ease us. It's gonna bear us down. . . . They was the time when we was on the lan'. They was a boundary to us then. . . . We was always one thing—we was the fambly—kinda whole and clear. An' now we ain' clear no more. . . . We're crackin' up, Tom. There ain't no fambly now" (536). She pleads with him to stay, and the family leaves the ranch. Ma's suspicion of any idea beyond that of loyalty to the family appears in her replying, when Tom insists that he must go, "You can't. . . . They wouldn' be no way to hide out. You couldn' trus' nobody. But you can trus' us. We can hide you, an' we can see you get to eat while your face gets well" (545–46).

A major change in attitude has occurred, however, by the time of the final interview between Tom and Ma. Young Ruthie Joad has undone the family by boasting about it. In a childish quarrel, she has revealed that her brother is a killer who is hiding nearby. Ma realizes then that Tom must go. While hiding, Tom has been thinking about Casy's ideas; and, when his mother says that she is worried that she may not know what has become of her son he tells her:

> "Well, maybe like Casy says, a fella ain't got a soul of his own, but on'y a piece of a big one—an' then. . . . Then it don' matter. Then I'll be all aroun' in the dark. I'll be ever'where—wherever you look. Wherever they's a fight so hungry people can eat, I'll be there. . . . An' when our folks eat the stuff they raise an' live in the houses they build—why, I'll be there" (572).

Tom has given up his concept of clan loyalty and has replaced it with the concept that one must help whoever needs help. Gradually the rest of the family comes to share this concept.

Pa learns the lesson of cooperation during the building of a dam to hold floodwater out of a cotton-pickers' camp; and he cries, "We can do her if ever'body helps" (595). Uncle John, too, finally breaks with tradition in order to teach the world a lesson. Instead of burying Rosasharn's stillborn baby, he sets it adrift in a creek, saying, "Go down in the street an' rot an' tell 'em that way. That's the way you can talk. Don' even know if you was a boy or girl. Ain't gonna find out" (609).

Most importantly, Ma's acceptance of the idea of a responsibility beyond the family after her last meeting with Tom is shown in her conversation with a neighbor whom she thanks for helping during Rosasharn's labor:

> The stout woman smiled, "No need to thank. Ever'body's in the same wagon. S'pose we was down. You'd give us a han'."
> "Yes," Ma said, "we would."
> "Or anybody."
> "Or anybody. Use' ta be the fambly was fust. It ain't so now. It's anybody. Worse off we get, the more we got to do." (606).

But while this speech accepts the spirit of Casy's idea of universal brotherhood, it does not translate the meaning into action. Some concluding gesture must indicate that education of the heart has transformed the family's behavior.

The opportunity arises in the barn where the family discovers the famished man. Ma's unstated suggestion that Rosasharn give her milk to him carries into practice the idea that "worse off we get, the more we got to do." Having come to the barn with almost nothing, the family, through Rosasharn, gives the one thing it has left to offer—the most intimate gift it could. The tableau in the barn does not halt an unfinished story; it marks the end of the story that Steinbeck had to tell about the Joads. Their education is complete; they have transcended familial prejudices. What happens to them now depends upon the ability of the rest of society to learn the lesson that the Joads have learned. The novel is neither riddle nor tragedy—it is an epic comedy of the triumph of the "holy spirit." The Joads have not been saved from physical privation, but they have saved themselves from spiritual bigotry.

The Grapes of Wrath is not, therefore, a period piece about a troublesome past era; it is an allegory applicable wherever prejudice and a proud sense of self-importance inhibit cooperation. The message of the novel is that cooperation can be achieved only when individuals of their own volition put aside special interests and work together to achieve a common purpose.

This message is not new in American literature. As Frederic Ives Carpenter pointed out not long after *The Grapes of Wrath* appeared, the novel reflects the thinking of the nineteenth-century American transcendentalists:

> Beside and beyond their function in the story, the ideas of John Steinbeck and Jim Casy possess a significance of their own. They continue, develop, integrate and realize the thought of great writers of American history. Here the mystical transcendentalism of Emerson reappears, and the earthy democracy of Whitman, and the pragmatic instrumentalism of William James and John Dewey. . . . Jim Casy translates American philosophy into words of one syllable, and the Joads translate it into action.[4]

Steinbeck's development of the vitally American thought of the transcendentalists does not indicate any specific "influence" of Emerson or Whitman. Neither Steinbeck nor Casy mention these past writers. Those who suppose that a younger man's ideas' paralleling and developing an older man's necessarily indicate a direct influence of the older on the younger make the very assumption that Emerson warned against—that we learn only from books. As Whitman suggested in "Song of Myself" two men may independently develop the same ideas from a sympathetic reading of Nature and observation of their fellowmen.

II

Structure and Meaning

The danger always exists, however, that readers will become so involved in the fortunes of the particular characters in a novel that its universal implications will be overlooked. To avoid this danger that *The Grapes of Wrath* might be interpreted as a unique story of one family's history, Steinbeck paired the chapters carrying forward the history of the Joads with others that show the general implications of the things that happened specifically to them.

Although the author nowhere in *The Grapes of Wrath* discusses the method he is using, he explains—as Peter Lisca indicates in *The Wide World of John Steinbeck*—the conscious literary theory behind his procedure in his preface to a book containing still pictures from the film, *The Forgotten Village,* Steinbeck's next creative project after *The Grapes of Wrath*. Commenting upon the problems that had

[4]Frederic I. Carpenter, "The Philosophical Joads," *College English,* II (January, 1941), 25.

to be faced in making this film about the introduction of scientific medicine to a remote, superstition-ridden Mexican community, the novelist explained:

> A great many documentary films have used the generalized method, that is, the showing of a condition or an event as it affects a group of people. . . . In *The Forgotten Village* we reversed the usual process. Our story centered on one family in one small village. We wished our audience to know this family very well, and incidentally to like it, as we did. Then, from association with this little personalized group, the larger conclusion concerning the racial group can be drawn with something like participation.[5]

In *The Grapes of Wrath*, Steinbeck did not take a chance on one method or the other; he used both to leave nothing undone that might help get his point across. The Joad story focuses, like *The Forgotten Village*, upon one family; and the "generalized method" is used in the interchapters. By using this double approach, Steinbeck did what he could to protect himself against the attacks some people made upon the book. By presenting the problems he was concerned with through the history of a particular family, he forced readers to visualize these problems as they affected individuals; and he denied escapists the consolation of the sociology textbook that treats depressed groups in numbers too large to be comprehended.

On the other hand, by using the generalized method, he denied in advance any charges that the history of the Joads was unique. By making what happened to the Joads representative of general situations that he also commented upon, he avoided the error made by some who attempted to answer his novel by presenting a unique case and suggesting that it was typical. In the device of the interchapter, Steinbeck found exactly the technique that he needed to make his novel simultaneously a general and an intensely personal history of the travails of a culture in transition.

Even this last description, however, too much limits the novel as a tale of a particular time and place. In a letter to his editor, Steinbeck observed that there are "five layers" in the book, although a reader finds no more than he has in himself. Steinbeck nowhere explains what "five layers" he has in mind, but an inquiry into his meaning might begin with the most famous explanation of "levels of meaning" in literature in Dante's *Convivio*:

[5]*The Forgotten Village* (New York, 1941), p. 5.

Exposition must be *literal* and *allegorical*. And for the understanding of this you should know that writings can be understood and must be explained, for the most part, in four senses. One is called *literal*; and this is the one which extends not beyond the letter itself. The next is called *allegorical*; and this is the one which is hidden beneath the cloak of these fables, being a truth concealed under pretty fiction. . . . The third sense is called *moral*; and this is the one which readers must ever diligently observe in writings, for their own profit and for that of their pupils. . . . The fourth sense is called *anagogical*, or supersensual; and this is when we expound spiritually a writing which, even in the letter, through the very things exprest expresseth things concerning eternal glory.[6]

We have examined already the literal and the allegorical levels of the novel as the literal tale of the migration from Oklahoma and as an illustration of the "education of the heart." On the "moral level," as I have also already suggested, the author—like Dickens— is expressing outrage that such conditions exist and pleading with readers to play their role in alleviating and eliminating them; the novel demands not agreement, but action. On the anagogic level, as Dante puts it, a writing expresses things "concerning eternal glory," a radiant security beyond the chaotic flux of man's material experiences. Does Tom Joad achieve a vision of such glory when he tells Ma that he'll "be all aroun' in the dark"? Does he urge the reader to aspire to a similar vision? Here the novel, with its rejection of traditional religious solutions, may provoke most thoughtful controversy.

Steinbeck speaks of a fifth layer. May individuality be transcended altogether? What of the "one big soul" that Casy feels everybody may be part of? What does Steinbeck mean when he speaks in chapter 14 of "Manself"? Are these concepts related to the "pure consciousness" sought through some meditation techniques? Is there a "layer" of experience at which individual distinctions are obliterated and at which life is perceived only as an all-pervasive force?

Contemplated in this manner, *The Grapes of Wrath* is not just a story of the Okies' migration to California, of man's perpetual

---

[6]Translation follows C. H. Grandgent, *Dante* (New York, 1916), 273–75. For a fuller account of Dante's arguments and their application to an analysis of the layers of meaning in *The Grapes of Wrath*, see the chapter on this novel by Warren French in *A Study Guide to Steinbeck: A Handbook to His Major Works,* edited by Tetsumaro Hayashi (Metuchen, N.J.; 1974).

pursuit of an elusive dream, of man's injustices to man, or even of the final reward of the deserving—the pure in heart that shall see God. It is rather the endless story of the strivings of a life-force to endure and triumph over inert obstacles that beset its way.

Steinbeck's Wine of Affirmation
in *The Grapes of Wrath*

by J. Paul Hunter

It has been a long time since John Steinbeck won the Drama Critics' Circle Award (1937) and the Pulitzer Prize (1939), and many of the critics who liked his work then have recently found little to praise. Since World War II, Steinbeck's new novels have received increasingly harsh reviews, and his critical reputation has declined steadily. Many of his most ardent admirers are now no longer confident that he will achieve the eminence once predicted for him, and some of them despair that he will ever do important work again. Now Steinbeck's decreasing stature seems to be reflected in another way—a growing tendency to find his later failures anticipated in his earlier work.

A few years ago it was popular to speculate on "what had happened" to Steinbeck, and some interesting answers were proposed: Steinbeck had lost touch with the country and with California, and the new urban and urbane life of New York was insufficient to fill his well; the death of Edward Ricketts (his close friend) had been such a personal blow to Steinbeck that his creative powers were affected; Steinbeck's ideology had changed, and the new Steinbeck had nothing to say; success had "spoiled" Steinbeck. However, even though some of these answers are still being given, an increasing number of critics seem to be turning to an answer given long ago by Steinbeck's detractors: that no decline in fact exists, that Steinbeck's talents, in his earlier period, were simply overrated by those who believed in the causes Steinbeck championed. One suspects that we may hear more and more of this point of view unless Steinbeck produces a new work of distinction. Once, much of the early work—certainly *The Grapes of Wrath* and *Of Mice and Men,* and possibly *In Dubious Battle* and several short pieces—seemed certain of a place in American fiction; now, it seems necessary to restate their claim to attention. Some of these pieces—especially the "worker" novels—are still taught in the college classroom, but already (despite the work of such critics as Peter Lisca and Warren French) there is danger of their becoming known as period pieces; again (as when it first appeared) Steinbeck's work needs to be defended as art rather than sociology.

I

Almost everyone agrees that *The Grapes of Wrath* is Steinbeck's most important early work, and it may well be that his critical reputation will ultimately stand or fall on that one book. Those who do not like the novel contend that it exemplifies Steinbeck's most blatant artistic weaknesses: lack of character development, imperfect conception of structure, careless working out of theme, and sentimentality. The last two chapters of the novel have been considered especially illustrative of these weaknesses, for they are said to demonstrate the final inability of Steinbeck to come to grips, except in a superficial way, with the ideological and artistic problems posed in the novel. The final scene has drawn the sharpest criticism of all, for here Steinbeck is charged with a sensational, shocking, and therefore commercial substitute for an artistic solution. The charges are not new ones, but they have a peculiar urgency at a time when the reputation of Steinbeck's early work is in danger of eclipse. And they constitute a basal attack on Steinbeck as artist, for if it is true that his most important book is inadequately conceived and imperfectly worked out, Steinbeck's claim to a place among significant novelists is seriously impaired.

The inadequacy of the ending of *The Grapes of Wrath*, is, however, more apparent than real. When the events of the last two chapters (and particularly the final scene in the barn) are examined in relation to the novel's total structure, they demonstrate a careful working out of theme in fictional terms. At the end, the Joads who remain (only six of the original twelve) seem to have a grim physical future; as they hover in a dry barn while the deluge continues and the waters rise, they face the prospect of a workless winter in a hostile world. But even though their promised land has turned out to be " 'no lan' of milk and honey' " but instead a battleground stained with the blood of Jim Casy, the Joads are at last able to come to grips with their world. Instead of idealists who dream of white houses and clusters of plenty they have become people of action who translate the prophecy of Jim Casy into the realities of wrath.

II

Under the old order in Oklahoma, the Joads were a proud people, individualists who asked nothing from anyone and who were content with their family-size world as long as they had a home surrounded by land which they could caress into fertility. Like the early Tom, they believed in " 'Just puttin' one foot in front a the other,' " and their thoughts did not stray beyond the limits of their families and their land. When the change comes, when they find themselves in captivity on land they have known as their own, and finally when the captor banks insult their dignity by driving them like nomads away from their homes, they do not understand the change, and they are helpless to oppose it. A few, like Muley Graves, may try, pitifully, to fight back with a sniper's bullet or a harassing laugh from parched fields, but the majority only know that the old is gone, and that they are powerless to fight against the new. As the dust covers the land and the burrowing machines cut their swath of progress through fields and houses, the men stand figuring in the dust, unbroken by events, but powerless to change them.

In their powerlessness, the Joads and their neighbors first choose the road of illusion, and they pursue their particular Western version of the American dream across Route 66. In their heads dance visions of plenty in California—their Canaan of the Golden West—but their map is an orange handbill, and soon their luxurious dreams of ripe fruit and white houses are changed to nightmares of hunger and Hoovervilles. Even in California, the Joads are merely individuals driven by forces they do not understand until, in wrath, they learn their lesson.

The lesson they learn forms the thematic base of *The Grapes of Wrath*, and although the Joads do not accept it fully until the end of the novel, the solution has been suggested quite early in the narrative. This theme—that strength can be achieved through a selfless unity of the entire community of Dispossessed—is first suggested when Tom and Jim Casy meet Muley Graves, a kind of mad prophet, on the old Joad place, and Muley is asked whether he will share his food. " 'I ain't got no choice in the matter,' " Muley says, then explains:

> "That ain't like I mean it. That ain't. I mean"—he stumbled— "what I mean, if a fella's got somepin to eat an' another fella's hungry—why, the first fella ain't got no choice. I mean, s'pose I pick up my rabbits an' go off somewheres an' eat 'em. See?
> "I see," said Casy. "I can see that. Muley sees somepin there Tom. Muley's got a-holt of somepin and it's too big for him, an' it's too big for me."

Though he still doesn't understand the concept fully, Casy has already incorporated Muley's prophetic wisdom into his own wilderness philosophy when, during his breakfast "grace" (two chapters later), he tells of his insights:

> "I got thinkin' how . . . mankin' was holy when it was one thing. An' it on'y got unholy when one mis'able little fella got the bit in his teeth an' run off his own way, kickin' an' draggin' and fightin'. Fella like that bust the holiness. But when they're all workin' together, not one fella for another fella, but one fella kind of harnessed to the whole shebang—that's right, that's holy."

Later Casy develops the idea and translates it into action, ultimately even sacrificing himself for it. But at first he finds few hearers. At breakfast, Ma is the only one who seems to notice the unusual "prayer," and she watches Casy "as though he were suddenly a spirit, not human any more, a voice out of the ground." The other Joads listen to Casy, but they do not hear him for a long time.

III

Casy's role is central to the structure of *The Grapes of Wrath*, for in him the narrative structure and the thematic structure are united. This role is best seen when set against the Biblical background which informs both types of structure in the novel. Peter Lisca has noted that the novel reflects the three-part division of the Old Testament exodus account (captivity, journey, promised land), but that the "parallel is not worked out in detail." Actually, the lack of detailed parallel seems to be deliberate, for Steinbeck is reflecting a broader background of which the exodus story is only a part.

Steinbeck makes the incidents in his novel suggest a wide range of Old and New Testament stories. As the twelve Joads (corresponding to the twelve tribes of Israel) embark on their journey (leaving the old order behind), they mount the truck in ark fashion, two by two:

> . . . the rest swarmed up on top of the load, Connie and Rose of Sharon, Pa and Uncle John, Ruthie and Winfield, Tom and the preacher. Noah stood on the ground looking up at the great load of them sitting on top of the truck.

Grampa (like Lot's wife) is unable to cope with the thought of a new life, and his wistful look at the past brings his death—a parallel emphasized by the scripture verse (quoting Lot) which Tom picks out to bury with Grampa. Uncle John (like Ananias) withholds money from the common fund, in order to satisfy his selfish desires. The list could be lengthened extensively, and many allusions are as isolated and apparently unrelated to the context as the ones cited here. Looked at in one way, these allusions seem patternless, for they refer to widely separated sections of Biblical history. However, the frequency of allusion suggests the basic similarity between the plight of the Joads and that of the Hebrew people. Rather than paralleling a single section of Biblical history, the novel reflects the broader history of the chosen people from their physical bondage to their spiritual release by means of a messiah.

If the reader approaches *The Grapes of Wrath* searching for too exact a parallel, he will be disappointed, for just when it seems as if a one-to-one ratio exists, Steinbeck breaks the pattern. Tom, for example, is a Moses-type leader of his people as they journey toward the promised land. Like Moses, he has killed a man and has been away for a time before rejoining his people and becoming their leader. Like Moses, he has a younger brother (Aaron-Al) who serves as a vehicle for the leader (spokesman-truck driver). And shortly before reaching the destination, he hears and rejects the evil reports of those who have visited the land (Hebrew "spies"—Oklahomans going back). But soon the parallel ends. Carried out carefully at the beginning, it does not seem to exist once the journey is completed. Granma, not Tom, dies just before the new land is reached, and Tom remains the leader of the people until finally (and here a different parallel is suggested) he becomes a disciple of Casy's gospel. This, in the miniature of one character, is what continually happens in *The Grapes of Wrath*. The scene changes, the parallel breaks; and gradually the context shifts from a basically Old Testament one to a New Testament one.

Steinbeck makes his allusions suggestive, rather than exhaustive, and he implies certain parallels without calling for too rigid an allegorical reading. In *East of Eden* Steinbeck also uses the method of suggestive allusion, and Adam's sons are not named Cain and Abel, but Caleb and Aaron (note the initials game again). This is no mere puzzle or covering of tracks, for the method serves to nullify too literal a reading, while at the same time drawing in a whole new range of suggestions. Instead of only Abel, the reader is asked to recall also the Biblical characteristics of another No. 2 brother. In *The Grapes of Wrath*, the method gives Steinbeck the freedom to skirt the particularly vexing time problem, for in the background myth the changes in the Hebrew people take place over centuries, while similar ideological changes in Steinbeck's characters occur within one year. In effect, Steinbeck collapses several hundred years of Hebrew history into the single year of his story; the entire history of man (according to the Judeo-Christian tradition) is reflected in the long hungry summer of one persecuted family.

This span of centuries is focused in Casy, whose ideas bridge the gap from Old to New Testament (according to the Christian concept of Biblical thought as developmental). Parallels between the life of Jim Casy and the messiah whose initials he bears are plentiful. He embarks upon his mission after a long period of meditation in the wilderness; he corrects the old ideas of religion and justice; he selflessly sacrifices himself for his cause, and when he dies he tells his persecutors, " 'You don' know what you're a-doin'.' " Less obvious perhaps, but equally important, is the role of the old Casy, before his wilderness experience, for he must ultimately be considered in messianic rather than Christological terms. Casy had been a typical hell-and-damnation evangelist who emphasized the rigidity of the old moral law and who considered himself ultimately doomed because human frailty prevented his achieving the purity demanded by the law. His conversion to a social gospel represents a movement from Old Testament to New Testament thought, an expanded horizon of responsibility. The annunciation of Casy's message and mission sets the ideological direction of the novel before the journey begins (just as the messiah concept influences Jewish thought for centuries before New Testament times), but only gradually does Casy make an impression upon a people (Jew-Joads) used to living under the old dispensation. Over Route 66 he rides quietly—a guest, a thirteenth—and only as time passes does the new idea blossom and the new order emerge; and the outsider—the thirteenth—becomes spiritual leader of a people to whom he had been a convention, a grace before meals.

Steinbeck's canvas is, on the surface, a painting of broad modern strokes, but its scenes are sketched along the outlines of the Judeo-Christian myth, a sort of polyptych depicting man's sojourn in a hostile world. The background is often faded, sometimes erased, and occasionally distorted, but structurally and ideologically it provides depth for Steinbeck's modern microcosm. In *The Grapes of Wrath* the background ideology becomes secularized and transcendentalized, but the direction of thought is still recognizable: a widening of concern. After the dispersion, there is still a saving remnant whose compassion begins to extend beyond its own familial or tribal group.

Steinbeck's method is perhaps not uniformly successful, and in some work done in this manner (such as *East of Eden* and *Burning Bright*) the fusion of the particular and the mythic seems, if not less perfectly conceived, less carefully wrought. But in *The Grapes of Wrath* the modern and mythic are peculiarly at one, and the story of a family which, in the values of its contemporary society, is hardly worth a jot, is invested with meaning when viewed against a history of enduring significance.

IV

Casy's gospel is reinforced thematically in *The Grapes of Wrath* by the panoramic intercalary chapters, which translate the plight of the Joad family into larger terms. Structurally, these chapters usually anticipate (in general terms) the particular actions which follow, and stylistically they often recall the King James Bible, particularly the prophetic books such as Isaiah and Jeremiah. Thematically, the most significant of these essays is Chapter 14, which begins:

The western land nervous under the beginning change. The Western States, nervous as horses before a thunder storm. The great owners, nervous, sensing a change, knowing nothing of the nature of the change.

Later the nature of the change is described:

One man, one family driven from the land; this rusty car creaking along the highway to the west. I lost my land, a single tractor took my land. I am alone and I am bewildered. And in the night one family camps in a ditch and another family pulls in and the tents come out. The two men squat on their hams and the women and children listen. . . . Here "I lost my land" is changed; a cell is split and from its splitting grows . . . "we lost *our* land." . . . Two men are not as lonely and perplexed as one. And from this first "we" there grows a still more dangerous thing: "I have a little food" plus "I have none." If from this problem the sum is "We have a little food," the thing is on its way, the movement has direction. Only a little multiplication now, and this land, this tractor are ours. . . . This is the beginning—from "I" to "we."

The intercalary chapters record this movement in the novel's action; similar passages in Chapters 1 and 29 (as Lisca has suggested) emphasize the change from family units to larger groupings:

1: The people came out of their houses. . . . Men stood by their fences. . . . The men were silent and they did not move often. And the women came out of the houses to stand beside their men—to feel whether this time the men would break. The women studied the men's faces secretly. . . . After a while the faces of the watching men lost their bemused perplexity and became hard and angry and resistant. Then the women knew they were safe and that there was no break.

29: The women watched the men, watched to see whether the break had come at last. The women stood silently and watched. And *where a number of men gathered together,* the fear went from their faces, and anger took its place. And the women sighed with relief, for they knew it was all right—the break had not come; and the break would never come as long as fear could turn to wrath. (Italics mine)

Though the movement from "I" to "we" is imaged several times throughout *The Grapes of Wrath*, the Joads do not really commit themselves to the new mode of thought until very late in the novel. Before their belated commitment, they show their limited view in many ways. Al cannot understand the men's cooperation in job-hunting: " 'Wouldn' it be better,' " he asks, " 'if one fella went alone? Then if they was one piece of work a fella'd get it,' " and he is told:

> "You ain't learned. . . . Takes gas to get roun' the country. Gas costs fifteen cents a gallon. Them four fellas can't take four cars. So each of 'em puts in a dime an' they get gas. You got to learn."

Rose of Sharon and Connie think only of themselves and of how they will break from the group, and when difficulties arise Connie wishes he had stayed in Oklahoma to man a tractor driving the people from the land. Later, alone, Rose of Sharon complains of her plight and frets about the coming child, and instead of sharing the family responsibility she adds to family worries. Uncle John is similarly preoccupied with his guilt and his personal problems and is almost useless to the group, picking cotton at only half the rate of the other men. Both he and Al withhold money from the family treasury. Noah, thoughtless of the others, wanders away. Connie, leaving a pregnant wife, also deserts. Even the children show a teasing selfishness. Ruthie eats her crackerjacks slowly so that she can taunt the other children when theirs is gone, and at croquet she ignores the rules and tries to play by herself.

Even though Ma, Pa, and Tom are less individualistic than the others, their concern is limited to the family group. Ma's one aim is keeping the family together, and when she says " 'This here fambly's goin' under,' " she is lamenting the disintegration of her entire world. While not a dynamic leader, Pa does his best to fulfill his patriarchal responsibility. Tom shows that he values the family over himself by breaking parole to make the journey with them, and he frequently demonstrates his dedication to them. Once, Tom wishes he could act like Al, but he is unable to forget his responsibility. Ma describes him well: " 'Everything you do is more'n you,' " she says.

Conversion to a wider concern comes rapidly toward the end of *The Grapes of Wrath*. Tom is the first Joad to extend his vision. In wrath, he moves to commitment beside the broken body of Jim Casy. A few days later, when he meets Ma in the dark cave, his dedication is complete. By contrast with Muley Graves (whose womb-like cave is an escape, a place where he feels " 'like nobody can come at me,' ") Tom does not plan to stay in his refuge. He tells Ma of his meditations about Casy and recites a passage Casy had quoted from Ecclesiastes (The Preacher):

"Two are better than one, because they have a good reward for their labor. For if they fall, the one will lif' up his fellow, but woe to him that is alone when he falleth, for he hath not another to help him up. . . . Again, if two lie together, then they have heat; but how can one be warm alone? And if one prevail against him, two shall withstand him, and a three-fold cord is not quickly broken."

Tom has to leave the family to protect them, but by now he also has a more important reason. He has seen the folly of a narrow family devotion like that of tractor-driver Willy Feely (" 'Fust an' on'y thing I got to think about is my own folks. What happens to other folks is their look-out.' ") and plans to work for a cause transcending family lines:

> "Tom," [Ma] said. "What you aimin' to do?"
> He was quiet for a long time. . . .
> "Tom," Ma repeated, "what you gonna do?"
> "What Casy done," he said.

Ma does not fully comprehend Tom's intention, but she has moved from a rigid defense of family unity during the journey (refusing to allow the family to split into two parts: " 'All we got is the family unbroke' ") to acceptance of new ideas in a new order. And after she leaves Tom she is tempted to reach backward—she takes "three steps toward the mound of vines"—but then quickly returns to the camp. Back in the boxcar, Pa talks wistfully of the past times (" 'spen' all my time a thinkin' how it use' ta be' "), but Ma is acclimated to the difference now. " 'This here's purtier—better lan',' " says Ma. Women, she observes, can adapt themselves to change. Earlier, before her meeting with Tom, she had lamented the breakup of the family; now she has a broader perspective: " '*People* is goin' on—changin' a little maybe, but goin' right on.' " Later, she is even more explicit. " 'Use ta be the fambly was fust. It ain't so now. It's anybody.' "

At the time of the birth, the larger unity is demonstrated. Pa (who had said earlier that he would work for twenty cents an hour even if it cost someone else his job) suddenly becomes a leader of men, conscious of the strength of organized effort:

> "Water's risin'," he said. "How about if we threw up a bank? We could do her if ever'body helped."

The dam is for the Joads, of course, but it is also for the others; all the families face the same danger, and each can flee—alone—or work together for their salvation, and they decide to stay:

> Over the men came a fury of work, a fury of battle. When one man dropped his shovel, another took it up.

Uncle John, choosing between desertion and devotion, works so hard that Pa has to caution him: " 'You take it easy. You'll kill yaself.' " And later, asked to dispose of the baby's body, Uncle John hesitates, then accedes:

> "Why do I got to do it? Why don't you fellas? I don' like it." And then, "Sure. I'll do it. Sure, I will. Come on give it to me." His voice began to rise. "Come on! Give it to me."

Al, whose only concern had been a good time, also moves toward what is, for him, an acceptance of larger responsibility (marriage to Aggie). Even Ruthie, on a child level, shows a change. On the way to the barn, she refuses to share the petals of her flower with Winfield, and, commanded to share, cruelly jabs one petal on his nose; but in her childish way she also senses that times are different:

> Ruthie felt how the fun was gone. "Here," she said. "Here's some more. Stick some on your forehead."

And, then, in Rose of Sharon, the final change.

V

Rose of Sharon's sacrificial act represents the final breakdown of old attitudes, and climaxes the novel's thematic movement. The final bastion of the old order, Rose of Sharon had been the most selfish of the remaining Joads; her concern had never extended beyond herself and her immediate family (Connie and the expected child). In giving life to the stranger (symbolically, she gives body and wine: Song of Songs 7:7—"Thy breasts [are like] to clusters of grapes"), she accepts the larger vision of Jim Casy, and her commitment fulfills the terms of salvation according to Casy's plan. In their hesitancy and confusion in the old times, the Joads had been powerless to change their fate. Unlike the turtle who dragged through the dust and planted the seeds of the future, they had drawn figures in the dust impotently with sticks. Now, however, they too are purposeful and share the secret of giving life.

The Biblical myth informs the final scene through a cluster of symbols which emphasize the change and affirm the new order. As the Joads hover in the one dry place in their world—a barn— the Bible's three major symbols of a purified order are suggested: the Old Testament deluge, the New Testament stable, and the continuing ritual of communion. In the fusion of the three, the novel's mythic background, ideological progression, and modern setting are brought together; Mt. Ararat, Bethlehem, and California are collapsed into a single unit of time, and life is affirmed in a massive symbol of regeneration.

The novel's final picture—a still life of Rose of Sharon holding the old man—combines the horror with the hope. Its imitation of the madonna and child (one face mysteriously smiling; the other wasted, and with wide, frightened eyes) is a grotesque one, for it reflects a grotesque world without painless answers, a world where men are hit by axe handles and children suffer from skitters. Steinbeck does not promise Paradise for the Joads. Their wildest dreams image not golden streets, but indoor plumbing. Dams will continue to break—babies will continue to be stillborn. But the people will go on: "this is the beginning—from 'I' to 'we.' " The grapes of wrath have ripened, and in trampling out the vintage the Dispossessed have committed themselves (like Casy) to die to make men free. In despair they learn the lesson; in wrath they share the rich red wine of hope.

The Grapes of Wrath:
An Achievement of Genius

by Peter Lisca

Steinbeck is frequently identified as a proletarian writer of the nineteen thirties, one whose dominant interest lay in the social and political problems of the Great Depression. But although *In Dubious Battle* and *Of Mice and Men* might generally seem to justify this reputation, neither work is specifically dated either by its materials or by Steinbeck's treatment. Migrant workers and union organizers had long been part of the California scene—and continued so to be. Steinbeck's early short story, "The Raid" (1934), dealing with two labor organizers, similarly avoids identification with its decade. It was not until 1939, at the very end of the period, that he published *The Grapes of Wrath*, a work clearly and specifically grounded in conditions and events that were then making news. In fact, so directly and powerfully did this novel deal with contemporary events that it itself became an important part of those events—debated in public forums, banned, burned, denounced from pulpits, attacked in pamphlets, and even debated on the floor of Congress. Along with such works as Upton Sinclair's *The Jungle* and Harriet Beecher Stowe's *Uncle Tom's Cabin, The Grapes of Wrath* has achieved a place among those novels that so stirred the American public for a social cause as to have had measurable political impact. Although thus associated with this class of social-protest fiction, *The Grapes of Wrath* continues to be read, not as a piece of literary or social history, but with a sense of emotional involvement and aesthetic discovery. More than any other American novel, it successfully embodies a contemporary social

"*The Grapes of Wrath*: An Achievement of Genius." From *John Steinbeck: Nature and Myth* by Peter Lisca (New York: Thomas Y. Crowell, Publishers, 1978), pp. 87–110. Copyright 1978 by Peter Lisca. Reprinted by permission of the publisher.

problem of national scope in an artistically viable expression. It is unquestionably John Steinbeck's finest achievement, a work of literary genius.

To appreciate fully this accomplishment, it is important to keep in mind Steinbeck's independence from the extensive literary and political proletarian movements of the period. He took no part in the organized efforts of writers, critics, and scholars to promote leftist or Communist theory as fulfillment of their responsibility to society; nor was he personally committed to any political viewpoint. While this kind of ideological neutrality enabled him to escape the pitfall of being too close to his materials—prejudice and propaganda—Steinbeck's intimate knowledge of his materials contributes greatly to the novel's realism and hence to its authority.

This familiarity had started while he was still a boy working on the farms and ranches surrounding his hometown of Salinas; it had grown through his college years during vacation and drop-out periods. More recently, in the autumn of 1936, he had written an article on migrant labor for *The Nation,* and a series of seven articles on these "Harvest Gypsies" for the *San Francisco News.* Steinbeck's fiction had early shown an absorbing interest in man's relationship to the land. He had explored it in terms of myth and biology in *To a God Unknown,* communally in *The Pastures of Heaven,* and as a factor of maturation in the short stories of *The Red Pony.* But through the field trips he made and the reading he did in preparation for his articles, and through subjecting himself personally to the migrant experience by living and working with the laborers, he was able to extend considerably the range of his terms to include the economic and, in the largest sense, the political. The truth of his observation in these latter dimensions of *The Grapes of Wrath* has long been substantiated by historians, sociologists, and political scientists; the truth of the novel's vision of humanity has been proven again and again in the hearts of its readers.

The novel's main characters are the twelve members of the Joad family: Grampa, Granma, Pa, Ma, their children Winfield, Ruthie, Noah, Al, Tom (just returned from prison), Rosasharn and her husband Connie, and Uncle John, joined by the ex-preacher Jim Casy. Dispossessed of their Oklahoma homestead by the banks having foreclosed the mortgage on their property, after the impoverished soil and dust storms made it impossible for them to support themselves, the group leaves for California, where they expect to find work as field hands. Meanwhile their land is joined to that of other unfortunate neighbors and worked with huge tractors. During the long journey the Joads find that they are part of a large migration of people with whom they share dangers and privations—especially the Wilson family. Grampa and Granma Joad die, and Noah leaves the group en route. The rest of them arrive in California to find the labor market glutted with families like themselves, resented and disliked by the inhabitants, exploited mercilessly by the large growers and oppressed by the police. Connie deserts the family; Jim Casy is arrested, appears later as a labor organizer but is killed by vigilantes, one of whom is in return killed by Tom, who then becomes a fugitive; Rosasharn's baby is born dead, and the novel ends with the Joads and their new friends, the Wainwrights, being even more hungry, ill, and impoverished than they were at the start.

All the characters are drawn as fully credible human beings, individual yet also representative of their social class and circumstances. This is true even of such clearly unusual and strong personalities as Tom Joad, Jim Casy, Ma Joad, and her daughter Rosasharn. Casy, although a vision-pierced prophet, retains enough elements of his revival-meeting, "Jesus-jumping" sect and cultural folkways to remain specifically human. Ma Joad's heroic maternal qualities reflect the strength and character of those migrant wives who not only survived but nourished as well their children and husbands. Steinbeck may have had these women especially in mind when he chose the title "Their Blood Is Strong" for the republication of his *San Francisco News* articles. Such details as Grampa's senility, Al's abilities as an automobile mechanic, Connie's faith in cheap, correspondence trade schools, Uncle John's guilt complex, and Rosasharn's pregnancy personalize each character in turn and contribute to the reader's involvement. But Steinbeck was not writing a novel of personal adventure and misfortune. His theme is the entire social condition of which his characters are a part, and it is primarily in terms of the total situation that they have existence. Thus their role is collective, representational of the Okies and migrant workers, just as in the novel the Shawnee Land and Cattle Company represents the evicting landlords, and the California Farmers' Association represents the growers.

That Steinbeck succeeds in creating characters capable of bearing such wide responsibility is a brilliant achievement, but the novel's vast subject requires even more. To have put the Joads into the large variety of situations needed to add up to a total picture would have destroyed their necessary credibility as particular and real people. Rather than vastly increasing the number of characters and thus weakening the reader's empathetic response and the novel's narrative line, or digressing from the action with authorial comment, Steinbeck conceived the idea of using alternating chapters as a way of filling in the larger picture. About one hundred pages, or one sixth of the book, is devoted to this purpose. At first glance it might seem that putting these digressions from the Joad family into separate chapters interrupts the narrative line even more, and that such a device breaks the book into two distinct parts, or kinds of chapters, resulting in a monotonous tick tock effect. Of this danger the author was well aware, and he avoided it by using in the interchapters a variety of devices to minimize their interruption of the narrative action, temper their expository nature, and otherwise blend the two kinds of chapters in the reader's mind.

Perhaps the most important of the devices Steinbeck uses is dramatization. Chapter five, for example, deals with the process by which mortgaged lands are taken over by the banks, the small farmers evicted, and these lands combined into vast holdings cultivated with efficient modern machinery by absentee landlords. Whereas such previous writers in the naturalist tradition as Theodore Dreiser and Frank Norris would have addressed the reader directly on these points, giving him a well-researched lecture, Steinbeck presents a series of vignettes in which, through generalized characters, situations, and dialogue, we see these things happening. The device is reminiscent of the medieval mystery plays which dramatized Bible stories and made them real to the common people; or of Greek drama which through familiar figures and a chorus of elders or women gave voice to the people's ethical and religious beliefs. Even the introduction and the transitions between these vignettes share this dramatized quality, as in the opening paragraph of chapter five, in which "owners" are presented walking, talking, touching things, and "tenants" are listening, watching, squatting in the dust which they mark with their little sticks, their wives standing in the doorways, the children wriggling their toes. In similar fashion other chapters present further aspects of the total situation: chapter seven, the buying of used cars for the trip; chapter nine, the selling of household goods; chapters seventeen and twenty-three, the nature of migrant life along the road.

Another device that Steinbeck uses to integrate the two kinds of material is juxtaposition. Of course, everything included in the interchapters is related to the events of the narrative. And each interchapter is so placed that its content is most pertinent to the action in the chapter that precedes or follows it. Highway 66 is the subject of the interchapter that follows the Joads' turning onto that highway; the rain and flood of chapter twenty-nine set the stage for the novel's conclusion. But furthermore, and most effectively, the interchapters are frequently used to develop or complete some specific action initiated in the preceding narrative, or vice versa. Chapter eight ends with the Joads driving off to sell their household goods; the interchapter that follows presents us with generalized characters selling just such goods; in chapter ten the Joads return with the empty truck, having sold their goods, pack the truck, and leave home; chapter eleven describes the gradual deterioration of an abandoned house. A variation of this device is achieved by repetition, in which some specific detail in one kind of chapter reappears in the other, thus further knitting the two together. The anonymous house in an interchapter becomes the Joad house when, in the following chapter, the latter also is seen with one of its corners knocked off the foundation; the anonymous man with a rifle who in the same interchapter threatens the tractor driver becomes Grampa Joad, who in the next chapter is reported to have shot out the headlight of a tractor.

To temper the expository nature of the interchapters and blend them with the rest, Steinbeck works with the prose style itself. The colorful folk idiom and figurative language used by the Joads, Wilsons, Wainwrights, and other migrants reappear in the dramatizations of the interchapters as the language also of the generalized characters. But (except for a brief oversight in chapter five) the conversation in the interchapters is not marked off by quotation marks, thus emphasizing its generalized nature and at the same time further blending it into other elements in these same chapters, weakening the identity and separateness of the more directly expository passages. Finally, through frequent variations in prose rhythm and idiom specifically pertinent to a particular scene, any tendency to group the expository chapters together as different in kind from the narrative ones is discouraged. Consider, for example, the variety of effects presented by chapter three on the turtle, chapter seven on the selling of used cars, chapter twenty-five on the California harvest.

There is, however, another important element of continuity in the prose style, in addition to the spoken idiom of its generalized characters. From the opening chapter, describing the drought, to the penultimate one, describing the flood with which the novel ends, the syntactical structures and rhythms of the narrative voice are those of the King James Bible: "The tractors had lights shining, for there is no day and night for a tractor and the discs turn the earth in the darkness and they glitter in the daylight." Almost disappearing in some of the chapters and totally possessing others, this voice, through its inescapable association with the Bible, becomes the moral center of the novel. It speaks with the force and authority of an Old Testament prophet, some Jeremiah haranguing a sinful people: "There is a crime here that goes beyond denunciation. There is a sorrow here that weeping cannot symbolize. There is a failure here that topples all our success. The fertile earth, the straight tree rows, the sturdy trunks and the ripe fruit. And children dying of pellagra must die because a profit cannot be taken from an orange."

All this is not to say that the sixteen interchapters are equally brilliant or successful. Perhaps three of them (nineteen, twenty-one, twenty-five), concerned with historical information, and a few paragraphs in two or three others, are too direct. But these are exceptions. For the most part, the problem raised by the use of interchapters is fully met by the brilliance of Steinbeck's literary technique.

In themselves, then, the interchapters accomplish several things for the novel. As has been mentioned, they provide an artistically acceptable place for the author's own statements, and they make possible the inclusion of additional materials without overusing the Joads or introducing many other specific characters. Closely related to this latter function is these chapters' capacity for amplification. They present dramatically with a sense of real experience what would otherwise be left to inference—that the situations and actions of the Joad family are typical of a large group of people, that the Joads are caught up in a problem of national dimensions. These are perhaps the chapters' most important uses. In addition, they provide information—the history of land ownership and migrant labor in California, for example. Also, through their depiction of American people, scenes, and folkways, there emerges the portrait of a substantial portion of a people—their political and religious beliefs, their music, manners, stories, jokes; their essentially pioneer character, with its virtues and its limitations. *The Grapes of Wrath* is a "great American novel" in every sense of that phrase.

The brilliance of conception and technique with which Steinbeck manages the larger units of his novel is equally evident in its small details. This is well illustrated by the migrants' frequent use of animals in their figures of speech, as natural to these people as literary references to professors of English. A tractor pushing over a shed "give her a shake like a dog shakes a rat"; Al, in his sexual pride, behaves like "a dung-hill rooster"; when all the Joads are forced to move into one house, Muley describes them as "piled in John's house like gophers in a winter burrow." Casy, the most intellectual of the Joad group, sometimes elaborates these simple figures of speech in his attempt to understand a new idea or express it to others—as when he envisions the socioeconomic forces in terms of a gila monster with its poison and its unbreakable hold, or compares the plight of the migrants to that of a bird trapped in an attic, trying to escape.

The narrative passages also make use of animals, but tend to employ them symbolically rather than figuratively. At the beginning of their journey the Joads' dog is killed on the highway by a "big swift car" which does not even stop. Another dog, the "lean brown mongrel . . . nervous and flexed to run" who upon sight of strangers "leaped sideways, and fled, ears back, bony tail clamped protectively" symbolized the conditions of the "Hooverville," a group of cardboard and tin shanties, in which his owner lives. A jackrabbit that gets smashed on the highway, lean gray cats, birds, snakes, and even bugs—all appear under perfectly natural circumstances and yet serve also as symbols. The most extended example of this is the turtle that is accorded the first interchapter entirely to itself. The indomitable life force that drives the turtle, the toughness that allows it to survive predators and trucks, the efficiency of nature that uses the turtle to unwittingly carry seeds and bury them, are clearly characteristic also of the Joads. They, too, carry their house (the truck) with them, survive the natural catastrophe of drought and flood and the intimidations of police and vigilantes; they, too, pick up life in one place and carry it to another. This correspondence is further strengthened when in the very next chapter Tom picks up a turtle as a present for the younger children, talks about turtles with Casy, and eventually releases it to travel—as the Joads are to do—southwest.

Steinbeck's use of machine imagery, though not so extensive, is similarly brilliant. As the first interchapter was devoted to the turtle, so the second is devoted mostly to the tractor, which through its blind power and lack of feeling comes to symbolize the impersonal industrialization and mechanization which, following the economic collapse of their family homestead, is bringing an end to the Joads' old way of life: "The driver . . . could not see the land as it was, he could not smell the land as it smelled; his feet did not stamp the clods or feel the warmth and power of the earth. . . . No man had touched the seed, or lusted for the growth. Men ate what they had not raised, had no connection with the bread. Behind the tractor rolled the shining disks, cutting the earth with blades—not plowing but surgery. . . . the long seeders— twelve curved iron penes erected in the foundry, orgasm set by gears, raping methodically, raping without passion." Not that Steinbeck in this chapter, or in the book, is symbolizing the evils of machinery, but rather the evils of its misuse. "Is a tractor bad? . . . If this tractor were ours it would be good. . . . If our tractor turned the long furrows of our land, it would be good. . . . We could love that tractor then. . . . But this tractor does two things—it turns the land and turns us off the land."

The tractor as symbol of a new era appears almost exclusively in the first part of the book; the most pervasive machine imagery is that of cars and trucks, from the shiny red transport which brings Tom home from prison to the broken-down jalopies of the migrants and the sleek new touring cars of the wealthy and the landowners. As a man used to be judged by the horse he rode, so now his social position is revealed by his car; as a man used to have to know about galls, chipped hooves, curb chains, saddle sores, he now must know about tires, valves, bearings, and spark plugs. "Funny how you fellas can fix a car. Jus' light right in an' fix her," Casy says to Tom and Al. "I couldn't fix no car, not even now when I seen you do it." "Got to grow into her when you're a little kid," Tom said. "It ain't jus' knowin'. It's more'n that." Survival, whether of man or animals, rests upon the ability to adapt to or master the new factors of environment. The Joads have this ability.

Even before the moment comes when they are to leave their home, they instinctively gather around the truck that is to carry them to California: "The house was dead, and the fields were dead; but this truck was the active thing, the living principle. . . . This was the new hearth, the living center of the family." From this beginning, through various tire punctures, flickering headlights, and boiling radiators, to the ending, in which "the old car stood, and water fouled the ignition wires and water fouled the carburetors," the condition of the Joads and their fellow migrants is the condition of their machines.

Powerful and unstinting as these machine images are in their reflection of the Joads' physical condition, there is developed at the same time a counterthrust which makes the novel a cry not of despair but of hope and affirmation. This thrust begins with Casy's early self-questioning and ends with Rosasharn breastfeeding a starving old man. The migrants journey west along Highway 66, but also along the unmapped roads of social change, from an old concept of community lost in the blowing dust of the opening chapter, or forfeited by foreclosed mortgages, to a new and very different sense of community formulated gradually on the new social realities. In an interchapter (seventeen), Steinbeck gives us this process in the abstract, and it is detailed in both kinds of chapters throughout the book.

Not all, however, can participate in this process. Muley Graves (a suggestive name) stays behind in Oklahoma, living in a cave like an animal because he cannot separate his sense of community and identity from the land and its history of personal experiences: "Place where folks live is them folks." As the generalized migrants in one of the interchapters express it to the buyers of their household goods, "You are not buying only junk, you're buying junked lives. . . . How can we live without our lives? How will we know it's us without our past?" Grampa Joad, like Muley, cannot bear to leave the land. He is given an overdose of painkiller and carried off it, but he does not make it beyond the Oklahoma border. Casy's little funeral speech assures the folks that "Grampa didn't die tonight. He died the minute you took 'im off the place. . . . Oh, he was breathin', but he was dead. He was that place, an' he knowed it. . . . He's jus' stayin' with the lan'. He couldn't leave it." As it is expressed in one of the interchapters, "This land, this red land is us; and the flood years and the dust years and the drought years are us."

The old sense of identity and community is invested not only in land and possessions, but in social customs and mores that also must be left behind; for example, traditional male and female roles. Ma Joad may be consulted briefly concerning food and space in the decision to include Casy in the family group, but once that decision is made she goes back to the house and womanly things. It is Casy who takes his place among the planning men grouped around Grampa, whose patriarchal headship must be acknowledged despite his senility. Similarly, when they take their places on the truck, Rosasharn, although pregnant, cannot sit in the cab on a comfortable seat: "This was impossible because she was young and a woman." The traditional distinction in social role is also evident in Ma's embarrassment at Casy's offer to salt down the pork. Ma "stopped her work then and inspected him oddly, as though he suggested a curious thing. . . . 'It's women's work,' she said finally." The preacher's reply is significant of many changes to come in the sense of community and the individual's changing role: "It's all work," he says. "They's too much of it to split up to men's or women's work." By the end of the book, the male role, deprived of its breadwinner status, loses also its authority. It is Ma Joad who, as woman and Earth Mother, becomes the nucleus of order and survival.

It is fitting that this break with domestic tradition should be announced by Casy, the spiritual leader of his community. He has already abandoned preaching the hell-fire, blood-of-the-Lamb evangelism which is typified in the book through the recollections of Pa Joad, when the spirit took him, "jumpin' an' yellin' " and Granma "talkin' in tongues." This primitive religion is also dramatically presented in Uncle John's sense of guilt and Mrs. Sandry's frightening of Rosasharn with predictions of the horrible penalties God visits on pregnant women who see a play or do "clutch-an'-hug dancin'." Significantly, during the happiest moment in the book, the dance at the federal migrant camp, "The Jesus-lovers sat and watched, their faces hard and contemptuous. They did not speak to one another, they watched for sin, and their faces condemned the whole proceeding."

Casy's new direction rejects such theological notions of sin ("There ain't no sin and there ain't no virtue. There's just stuff people do."); it defines the religious impulse as human love ("What's this call, this sperit? . . . It's love."); and it identifies the Holy Spirit as the human spirit in all mankind ("Maybe all men got one big soul ever'body's a part of"). Casy joins the migration not to escape or to preach but to learn from the common human experience: "I'm gonna work in the fiel's, in the green fiel's, an' I'm gonna try to learn. . . . why the folks walks in the grass, gonna hear 'em talk, gonna hear 'em sing. Gonna listen to kids eatin' mush. Gonna hear husban' an' wife poundin' the mattress in the night. Gonna eat with 'em an' learn." What Casy finally learns, in jail after giving himself up to save Tom and Floyd, is that man's spiritual brotherhood must express itself in a social unity, which is why he becomes a labor organizer. The grace that he reluctantly says before eating his first breakfast with the Joads is already groping in that direction: "I got to thinkin' how we was holy when we was one thing, an mankin' was holy when it was one thing. An it on'y got unholy when one mis'able little fella got the bit in his teeth an run off his own way, kickin' an' draggin' an fightin'. Fella like that bust the holiness. But when they're all workin' together, not one fella for another fella, but one fella kind of harnessed to the whole shebang—that's right, that's holy." It is for this belief in a new sense of community that he gives his life, rediscovering for himself his American heritage of Thomas Paine's *The Rights of Man,* Ralph Waldo Emerson's "The Over Soul," Walt Whitman's *Democratic Vistas.*

Although varying considerably in their ability to share Casy's spiritual vision, it is the Joads' growing acceptance of the social application of that vision that gives them and the other migrants their strength to endure and their faith in a better future. Even Muley knows why he must share his stringy wild rabbit with Tom and Casy: "What I mean, if a fella's got somepin to eat an' another fella's hungry—why, the first fella ain't got no choice." Mrs. Wilson's answer to Ma Joad's thanks for help puts it differently: "People needs [have the need] to help." A few pages later, Ma Joad's reply to Mrs. Wilson's thanks for help gives the concept a further turn: "You can't let help go unwanted." It is significant that the first example of spontaneous sharing with strangers on the journey is a symbolic merging of two families: Grampa's death in the Wilsons' tent, his burial in one of their quilts with a page torn from their Bible; Ma Joad's promise to care for Mrs. Wilson. As Pa Joad expresses it later, "We almost got a kin bond." Near the end of the novel, Al Joad tears down the tarpaulin that hangs between themselves and the Wainwrights, so that "the two families in the car were one." In one of the most hauntingly beautiful scenes of the book, a family spontaneously shares their breakfast with a stranger (Tom), and their hard-found paying job as well, even though this shortens the time between themselves and starvation.

Consider in contrast the Joads' neighbor who turned tractor driver: "I got a wife an' my wife's mother. Them people got to eat. Fust an on'y thing I got to think about is my own folks." Ma Joad herself starts out on the journey with a ferocious defense of her own family against all things, because "All we got is the fambly"; four hundred pages later she has learned, "Use' ta be the fambly was first. It ain't so now. It's anybody. Worse off we get, the more we got to do." Tom Joad has learned in prison to mind his own business and to live one day at a time. As he puts it, "I'm just puttin' one foot in front a the other," and again a few pages later, "I ruther jus' lay one foot down in front a the other"; in another image, "I climb fences when I got fences to climb." By the end of the book he says, "But I know now a fella ain't no good alone"; and he goes out dedicated to work for the improvement of his people, though it may mean his own death: "Then it don't matter. Then I'll be ever'where—wherever you look. Wherever there's a fight so hungry people can eat, I'll be there."

These are only a few of the particulars that key into chapter seventeen's most abstract statement: "They shared their lives, their food, and the things they hoped for in the new country. . . . twenty families became one family, the children were the children of all." The family of man is established, the change from "I" to "we," the new sense of identity and community through which the people survive. Those who do not share, who continue selfish and distrustful, "worked at their own doom and did not know it."

Of all the abstract statements, generalized examples, and specific acts addressed to this principle of survival, Steinbeck saved the most powerful for the novel's concluding scene. In Rosasharn's feeding of a stranger with the milk from her own breast is reenacted the primal act of human nourishment and the most intimate expression of human kinship. That the stranger is an old man and that, for physical reasons, Rosasharn is glad to give the milk, which continues to gather painfully in her breast although her baby is dead, make its symbolic assertion all the stronger. The significance of this final act is further magnified by the facts that the old man is weak from giving his share of the food to his son, and that the son had "stoled some bread" for him but the father had "puked it all up." The ultimate nourishment is the sharing of oneself, as Rosasharn symbolizes by literally giving of her body. This act takes on religious overtones by the still, mysterious, and lingering quality of the scene as "her lips came together and smiled mysteriously" (the last words of the novel), suggesting a common subject of religious paintings—the Madonna nursing her child whom she knows to be the Son of God.

These overtones do more than enhance a humanistic symbol, however. They bring to conclusion a whole level of the novel that exists in religious terms beginning with the title itself, *The Grapes of Wrath*, a phrase from "The Battle Hymn of the Republic" that alludes to the Book of Revelation in the Bible, containing prophecies of the coming Apocalypse: "And the angel thrust in his sickle into the earth, and gathered the vine of the earth, and cast it into the great winepress of the wrath of God." The reference is reinforced in one of the novel's interchapters: "In the souls of the people the grapes of wrath are filling and growing heavy, heavy for the vintage." From this beginning, the Biblical allusions follow thick and fast, for Steinbeck enlarges the significance of his Okies' experiences by associating them with those of the Israelites (the chosen people) in the Old Testament and thus suggesting their human and historical importance. Although not formally so divided, the novel falls into three parts: the drought and dispossession (chapters 1–11), the journey (chapters 12–18), and the arrival in California (chapters 19–30). This corresponds respectively to the oppression and bondage of the Israelites in Egypt, their Exodus and wandering in the wilderness, and their entrance into the Land of Canaan. The plagues in Egypt, which released the Israelites, have their parallel in the drought and erosion in Oklahoma; the Egyptian oppressors, in the bank officials; the hostile Canaanites, in the equally hostile Californians. In both accounts the Promised Land is first glimpsed from a mountain top. As there were twelve tribes of Israel, so are there twelve Joads (counting Rosasharn's husband). Even the family name recalls a parallel—the tribe of Judah, or the Jews. Ma Joad's simple faith that "We're the people," is reminiscent of the Jewish faith in God's promise that the Jews are a chosen people, as expressed in Psalm Ninety-five: "For He is the Lord our God; and we are the people of his pasture, and the sheep of his hand." As the Jews formulated new codes of law by which they governed themselves in their Exodus (see the Book of Deuteronomy), so the migrants evolve new codes of conduct (see chapter seventeen). When Uncle John sets Rosasharn's baby in an apple box among the willow stems of a stream, saying, "Go down an' tell 'em," it is the counterpart of Moses in a basket among the bulrushes. A Negro spiritual completes the allusion for the reader: "Let my people go." These are but a scattered sampling of the many, often quite specific parallels through which Steinbeck—in addition to the recurring Biblical prose style mentioned earlier—sustains in the novel a strong religious presence.

The Biblical parallels of three of the novel's characters, however, are [sic] of such significance and complexity that they require further discussion—Casy, Tom, and Rosasharn. Jim Casy is, as his initials suggest, in several ways a Christ figure. He breaks with the old religious beliefs and practices, of which he was an advocate, and after a retreat "in the hills, thinkin', almost you might say like Jesus went into the wilderness," emerges to preach an initially unpopular new testament, rejecting a god of vengeance for an oversoul of love. "You can't hold no church with idears like that," Tom tells him. "People would drive you out of the country. . . ." He dedicates himself to establishing his "church" among the people and is killed uttering as his last words a paraphrase of Christ's "They know not what they do": "You don' know what you're a-doin' "; Tom, who has been a doubter all along, now announces himself as Casy's disciple. It all fits together very neatly, too neatly. Steinbeck, however, like other modern American writers, such as Faulkner, is not content to use elements of Christian myth on the simple level of allegory. Thus Casy's Christ role is deliberately confused in two ways. First, he is given attributes of John the Baptist, such as the description of his speech as "a voice out of the ground," and, of course, his role as a baptizer. One of those he clearly remembers baptizing is Tom Joad, and thus the second area of confusion.

For Tom Joad, too, beginning with his baptism by Casy, is given the attributes of a Christ figure. He is even called "Jesus Meek" by his fellow prisoners because of his grandmother's Christmas card with that phrase on it. Once when he seems to be rebelling against his emerging role and says he wants to "go out like Al. . . . get mad like Pa. . . . drunk like Uncle John," his mother shakes her head. "You can't, Tom. I know. I knowed from the time you was a little fella. You can't. They's some folks that's just theirself an' nothin' more. . . . Ever'thing you do is more'n you. . . . You're spoke for." In other words, his succession to the role of Christ the Messiah, or Saviour, is complete when, in a scene rife with womb imagery (mother, cave, food, darkness), Tom is figuratively reborn and tells his mother of his vocation to preach and live the words of Casy. His speech, quoted in small part above (page 106), paraphrases the words of Christ recorded in Luke 4:18 and Matthew 7:3 and 25:35–45, as well as in Isaiah 65:21–22: "And they shall build houses and inhabit them, they shall not build and another inhabit; they shall not plant and another eat." Tom Joad is a complex figure, and it is possible to see in him also sufficient attributes (a specific act of violence, for example) to identify him as a type of Moses who will lead his people to a better future, or the apostle Paul, particularly in the specific details of his conversion.

Though not so rich a figure, Rosasharn also gathers to herself multiple Christian aspects. To begin with, her real name, Rose of Sharon, from the Song of Solomon ("I am the Rose of Sharon, and the lily of the valleys") is frequently interpreted as referring to Christ. The Song of Solomon also contains the line, "This thy stature is like to a palm tree, and thy breasts to clusters of grapes." Thus the final scene in which she feeds the old man with her milk is symbolic of the Eucharist: "Take, eat, this is my body. . . ." Through this identification, the anonymous old man becomes Grampa Joad, whose image for the plenty of California had been a "big bunch a grapes" which he could squash on his face until the juice ran down his chin. As both Christ and Madonna figures, Rosasharn combines attributes more divergent than does Casy (Christ and John the Baptist) or even Tom (Moses, Christ, Saint Paul).

Probably because of this very diversity of reference, these three characters greatly contribute to the lively tension of Biblical allusions in the novel's prose style, events, and structure. The novel never falls into allegory. Furthermore, and more important, they bring together and make one in their lives the novel's social message and certain precepts of Christianity. Whether *The Grapes of Wrath* as a whole promulgates specifically Christian values is a moot point depending entirely on one's definition of what is essentially Christian. Both sides have been well argued. There is no question, however, that through the abundance, variety, and intensity of its Biblical allusions the novel imbues its social message with a religious fervor and sanction.

When *The Grapes of Wrath* was published in 1939, one reviewer said that it seemed to him "as great a book as has yet come out of America." The passing of time has given no reason for correcting that estimate.

The Grapes of Wrath
as Heroic Fiction

by Leonard Lutwack

The line of descent from *The Octopus* to *The Grapes of Wrath* is as direct as any that can be found in American literature. The journey of the Okies in Steinbeck's book is certainly in the spirit of one of those "various fightings westward" that Norris identified as productive of epic writing: "Just that long and terrible journey from the Mississippi to the ocean is an epic in itself."[1] As one would expect, too, the later book reflects a more advanced stage of economic development, presenting as it does the struggle of proletarian masses against capitalist power, while the conflict in *The Octopus* is between two parties of the owning class, the ranchers, or small entrepreneurs, against the trust. Both novels have a universalizing tendency in that they create from a local situation a synecdoche of worldwide import. Thus Steinbeck's Okies, having all the surface characteristics of rural Americans of a certain region, are essentially farmers suddenly reduced by natural catastrophe and economic process to the status of unskilled laborers. Theirs is a cataclysmic predicament of the twentieth century. In the course of the journey imposed upon them they learn to identify themselves as a separate class and then to discover and develop leaders who will guide them in their effort to reestablish themselves in society. *The Grapes of Wrath* is a thoroughly didactic epic novel: an exploited group discovers that it is being exploited, that it is, indeed, a new class in society, the proletariat; individuals within that class discover the manner of that exploitation and grope for the means to combat it, or at least protest it; and the

[1]"A Neglected Epic," *The Responsibilities of the Novelist* (New York, 1928), p. 281.

reader of the book, presumably, discovers that an alarming world economic condition is now making itself felt in America. The novel has a two-part theme, the education of a people and the education of its emerging leaders, and a three-part action, the dispossession, migration, and resettlement of a people.

To dignify his starving sharecroppers and give form to their story, Steinbeck draws upon two epic traditions of migratory peoples, the account of the Israelites in the Book of Exodus and the story of the Trojans in the *Aeneid*. From the New Testament and the epic tradition he derives the forms of heroism and self-sacrifice that inspire the leaders of these people. Criticism has taken more note of the Bible influence because it is so obvious: there are unmistakable parallels between the trials of the Okies and the Israelites, between preacher Casy and Christ, and between Tom Joad and Moses. It is not surprising that Steinbeck's language is a close imitation of the English of the King James Version. A result of his deliberate effort to adapt style to subject in all his works, it constitutes a much more successful solution to the problem of creating a special style for an epic novel than Norris's romantic colors in *The Octopus*. To obtain elevation of style Steinbeck poeticizes his prose by echoing the phrasing and vocabulary of the King James Version in his descriptive passages and, secondly, by endowing the low-colloquial speeches of Casy and Tom Joad with an unusual amount of passion, imagery, and philosophical comment. As an example of the first method, here is the opening paragraph of chapter 17, one of the interchapters:

> The cars of the migrant people crawled out of the side roads onto the great cross-country highway, and they took the migrant way to the West. In the daylight they scuttled like bugs to the westward; and as the dark caught them, they clustered like bugs near to shelter and to the water. And because they were lonely and perplexed, because they had all come from a place of sadness and worry and defeat, and because they were all going to a new mysterious place, they huddled together; they talked together; they shared their lives, their food, and the things they hoped for in the new country. Thus it might be that one family camped near a spring, and another camped for the spring and for company, and a third because two families had pioneered the place and found it good. And when the sun went down, perhaps twenty families and twenty cars were there.[2]

[2]*The Grapes of Wrath* (New York, 1939), p. 264.

Employing Biblical devices more thickly than most, this passage indicates what Steinbeck is seeking to do and the means he uses. Dignity and solemnity are imparted to the miserable plight of the Okies by triadic phrasing, augmentations such as "near to" and "it might be," repetitions of word and phrase, and exact echoes such as "found it good." Association with the Bible story of the Israelites through language alone lends considerable elevation to the Okies. In his second method of aggrandizing the prose style of his novel, Steinbeck tries to intensify with poetic expressiveness the crude speech of his Okies. The result, as illustrated in an informal sermon by Casy, resembles the style of Huck Finn in his lyrical moments:

> "I ain't sayin' I'm like Jesus," the preacher went on. "But I got tired like Him, an' I got mixed up like Him, an' I went into the wilderness like Him, without no campin' stuff. Nighttime I'd lay on my back an' look up at the stars; morning I'd set an' watch the sun come up; midday I'd look out from a hill at the rollin' country; evenin' I'd foller the sun down. Sometimes I'd pray like I always done. On'y I couldn' figure what I was prayin' to or for. There was the hills, an' there was me, an' we wasn't separate no more. We was one thing. An' that one thing was holy." (P. 110)

Between these two extremes, the thick Biblical and the poetic low colloquial, lies the narrative style in which the bulk of the Joads' story is told. It retains some of the deliberate rhythm of the Biblical and some of the realistic vocabulary of the colloquial styles. The three styles make a blend, one style modulating well with another. There is no weakness in the book on that score, but there is some question about the appropriateness of the exalted styles altogether. Just as in the ritual behavior of the Okies, so in the exalted language that describes them and in the impassioned speech that they sometimes use, there is considerable pompousness. In both gesture and speech Steinbeck occasionally comes too near to a burlesque tone; his seriousness becomes excessive, and he commits the prime error of many writers who attempt the epic, swelling and grandioseness. He lifts the Joads, in particular, and the Okies, in general, too quickly and abruptly from their realistic existence to the level of epic heroism.

There is no question of the influence of the Old and New Testaments on *The Grapes of Wrath*. Parallels with the *Aeneid* are hardly as deliberate, but are worth pointing out as evidence that the whole ancient heroic tradition contributes to the materials of the epic novel. In the American work the three-part narrative scheme of the *Aeneid* appears again in the record of a people who lose their homeland, make a perilous journey to a promising new land, and fight against the hostile natives there for a chance to begin a new life. The first two parts are more tightly woven than the third because the family stays very close together as they leave home and travel the road across the country, but after their arrival in California the pressures pulling them apart multiply. Uncle John's guilt gets worse, Rosasharn's time is drawing near, Al's desire to strike out for himself is intensified, the youngsters Ruthie and Winfield are less controllable, Casy and Tom are being drawn into the larger community. The Joad family's mode of travel, the improvised car-truck piled high with household goods, can no longer serve as a striking central image after the journey is over and the family lives in a more complicated social setting. The result of all this individual stress and social complication is an increased variety of material and a more episodic structure in the third part of the novel. There is still a strong line of action in the economic struggle, but it does not have the clear goal of the earlier drive towards freedom in the West. The same blurring of the narrative line, the same sense of confused action, is to be noted in the last part of the *Aeneid*; but whereas this falling-off of intensity is a fault in the *Aeneid* because it does not accord with the triumph of Trojan arms, in the novel it is in perfect accord with the frustration of Okie ambitions. Undoubtedly, interest in the third part of the *Aeneid* flags because attention is turned away from sharply focused individuals, Aeneas himself and Dido, to more generalized accounts of tribes and warring nations. Similarly, in *The Grapes of Wrath* the exclusive interest in the family sustains the first two parts better than the last part, in which there is a scattering of interest among larger social units.

Narrative structure is the most accomplished aspect of *The Grapes of Wrath*. Steinbeck achieves a successful solution to the chief structural problem of the epic writer, whether it be Homer or Tolstoy: the harmonization of the general social action involving masses of people and major issues with particular actions involving closely examined individuals and their concerns. Steinbeck simplifies his problem somewhat by restricting himself to the members of one family and their few close associates, Casy and the Wilsons, and to a few quickly drawn agents of their enemies.

His Joads serve the same synecdochic purpose of Zola's Maheus in *Germinal,* but it is to be noted that Zola does not confine himself to one side of the struggle alone nor to one family of miners. The Joads exemplify in detail what is presumably going on in thousands of similar families. Moreover, Steinbeck supplies a more explicit link between the general and particular actions by using "interchapters" or panoramic narrative in which the activities of all the Okies are summarized, sometimes from an objective viewpoint and sometimes as collective monologue from the viewpoint of representative Okies. Enough details are common to both kinds of action to give the sense that the Joads are living the same kind of life and having the same thoughts and feelings as the masses described in the interchapters. Except for the interruption they make in the story of the Joads, the interchapters are readily assimilated for their thematic and material relevance.

A few minor echoes from classical epics may be cited. The patriarch of the family whose fortunes we follow, the Joads, has to be carried onto the truck when they are forced to leave home; he dies on the way, and a pause in the journey is made to bury him with solemn rites in a strange land. After the feast of pork and potatoes, Ma Joad declares, "Grampa—it's like he's dead a year." A granddaughter consoles the dead man's grieving old wife; she lies "beside the old woman and the murmur of their soft voices drifted to the fire" where the men were sitting. At the place where Grampa dies the Joads make friends with another family of Okies, the Wilsons, whose car has broken down. The two Joad boys undertake to repair it and they find the necessary parts in an auto graveyard presided over by a one-eyed "specter of a man," who cries miserably as he tells them his sad plight. This scene, according to an early commentator on Steinbeck, "afterwards floats in the mind like a piece of epic."[3] The car is repaired and the two families now join forces as they proceed on their journey together. These are but faint echoes of the story of Aeneas's father, Aeneas at Eryx, and Odysseus's tale of Polyphemus.

The ceremonial solemnity with which the Joads perform certain family functions suggests a more general epic quality. The frequent family councils, the ritual killing of the pigs before the departure, the burial of Grampa, and many other activities are executed by Steinbeck's American sharecroppers with all of the

[3] Harry T. Moore, *The Novels of John Steinbeck* (Chicago, 1939), p. 71.

ponderous care and sacred protocol of noblemen out of the heroic tradition of the past. Such attempts to aggrandize the folk, also to be found in *The Octopus* and *For Whom the Bell Tolls,* often fall into bathos in Steinbeck. Much more effectively done are the many prophecies of disaster uttered all along the road to California, particularly one by a kind of Teiresias whom the Joads meet in one of the improvised campsites. A "ragged man," his coat a mass of "torn streamers," he at first refuses to say what lies in store for the Joads in California. "I don' wanna fret you," he tells Pa. What he finally does reveal is exactly what happens to the Joads in the remaining half of the book—their being exploited in an economic situation in which thousands of men compete for a few jobs. He finishes his prophecy, "and then he turned and walked quickly away into the darkness."

Jim Casy is a prophet in another, more hopeful, tradition, that of Christ in the New Testament. Disturbed by the economic plight of the farming class he serves as a Baptist preacher, he makes a retreat in order to ponder their situation and decides that he cannot help by continuing in the ministry. Actually, his Christianity is simply broadened by the sudden growth of his social consciousness. He becomes inspired with the idea that the brotherhood of all men must work together for social justice, and to this he adds a more abstract idea of the holy relatedness of mankind in a kind of Emersonian oversoul.[4] This doctrine he preaches as a new revelation to save the Okies from destruction and the world from economic warfare. He dies preaching for the cause and saying to his assailants, "You don' know what you're a-doin!" But he leaves behind a disciple in Tom Joad, who at once begins to tell the story of Casy and even thinks he sees him after his death.

If Casy is Christian and socialist, Ma Joad is pagan and primitive. If Casy adds the spirit of a New Testament prophet to the doctrine of a twentieth-century class-conscious revolutionary, Ma Joad is in the ancient tradition of the kore-goddess protecting her hero-son and her people. She is splendidly revealed (*dea certe*) to Tom when he returns home, a stranger, after spending four years in prison for having killed a man in a quarrel:

> Her full face was not soft; it was controlled, kindly. Her hazel eyes seemed to have experienced all possible tragedy and to have

[4]Steinbeck's Emersonian transcendentalism is carefully worked out by Peter Lisca in *The Wide World of John Steinbeck* (New Brunswick, N. J., 1958), pp. 168–69.

mounted pain and suffering like steps into a high calm and a superhuman understanding. She seemed to know, to accept, to welcome her position, the citadel of the family, the strong place that could not be taken.... And from her great and humble position in the family she had taken dignity and a clean calm beauty. From her position as healer, her hands had grown sure and cool and quiet; from her position as arbiter she had become as remote and faultless in judgment as a goddess.

She moved toward him lithely, soundlessly in her bare feet, and her face was full of wonder. Her small hand felt his arm, felt the soundness of his muscles. And then her fingers went up to his cheek as a blind man's fingers might. And her joy was nearly like sorrow.... (Pp. 100–101)

The only embrace between mother and wandering son is the touch of her hand to his face; between mother-goddess and human son is the same gulf that we see between Venus and Aeneas in book one of the *Aeneid*: "Oh, why may we not join/Hand to hand, or ever converse straightforwardly?" Like Pilar in *For Whom the Bell Tolls*, like Dilsey in *The Sound and the Fury*, Ma Joad is richly endowed with the awesome, divine presence of the goddess who presides over the generations of the family and the cycle of life. Her every action—except one, as we shall see—is motivated by the instinctive desire to keep the family together for the purpose of mere survival. She cradles the dying Granma Joad in her arms, she protects and nourishes her pregnant daughter, she restores her son Tom to life.

Produced by the influences of a Christ-like companion, Casy, and his mother-goddess, Tom Joad is indeed a hero of divine origin. He is moved to heroic acts by the spirit of anger and revenge which the murder of Casy stirs in him, and on the other hand by the spirit of compassion and love for mankind which his mother so well demonstrates in her selfless devotion to the family. Images of death and rebirth mark Tom's relations with Casy and Ma Joad, as in their different ways they strive to bring him to the role of a hero. There is something terribly grim and sad about the career of Tom. Never allowed a romantic interlude, he is plunged into the troubles of his people upon his return from prison and slowly comes to an awareness of his responsibilities of leadership. Almost glumly, with little expression of personal feeling, he does not only what is expected of him but more besides. A peak in his development occurs when, in the manner of a classic brother-in-arms, Tom at once kills the strikebreaker who has killed Casy; Tom is then himself struck, escapes from his pursuers, and comes to an irrigation ditch, where he bathes his torn cheek and nose. Casy, when he was a preacher, used to baptize people in irrigation ditches; he is killed as he stands beside a stream. Tom's introduction to the bitter struggle of worker against producer dates from the violent experience beside the stream. The stinging baptism at the irrigation ditch, after he has fled, does not lead him into his new life at once, however. He must die before he can be wholly reborn, and he must make a retreat to consecrate himself to the cause in his soul as well as in his arms and receive the blessing of his goddess-mother as well as the example of his surrogate father. He rejoins the family, but because he is being sought by the police and can easily be identified by his wounds, he must remain hidden: he is as one who no longer exists in the Joad family. To get past the guards who are looking for him, he lies between two mattresses in the Joad truck, and then he takes refuge in the brush near the boxcar that the family is now inhabiting. After Ruthie has told her playmates about her big brother Tom, Ma decides that she must release Tom from his obligation to the family for his own safety, and she goes to the "cave of vines" he has improvised. Tom, in the meantime, has come around to a sense of his duty to "fight so hungry people can eat" and is ready to begin a new life away from the family.

The scene in which Ma and Tom part is the climax of Tom's career as a hero and the very heart of Steinbeck's point that class must replace family as the social unit worth fighting for. It is a high point in Steinbeck's writing, and some of its strength comes from the association of rebirth imagery and myths of the mother-goddess and her hero son with the crude story of an organizer of farm labor in twentieth-century America. Carrying a dish of "pork chops and fry potatoes," Ma walks at night "to the end of the line of tents" in the camp of fruit pickers and steps "in among the willows beside the stream" until she reaches "the black round hole of the culvert where she always left Tom's food." She leaves her package at the hole and waits a little distance away, among the willows:

> And then a wind stirred the willows delicately, as though it tested them, and a shower of golden leaves coasted down to the ground. Suddenly a gust boiled in and racked the trees, and a cricking downpour of leaves fell. Ma could feel them on her hair and on her

shoulders. Over the sky a plump black cloud moved, erasing the stars. The fat drops of rain scattered down, splashing loudly on the fallen leaves, and the cloud moved on and unveiled the stars again. Ma shivered. The wind blew past and left the thicket quiet, but the rushing of the trees went on down the stream. (P. 567)

A "dark figure" finally appears at the culvert; it is Tom and after her plea to talk with him he leads Ma to his hideout, across a stream and a field filled with "the blackening stems" of cotton plants. Ma crawls into the "cave of vines" and there in the dark they talk. She explains that she did not let him go earlier because she was afraid for him; with the touch of her hand she discovers that he has a bad scar on his face and his nose is crooked. Again, as in the first scene of recognition between mother and son, the hand of the mother lingers lovingly on the face of the son, just as Thetis "took her son's head in her arms" before she releases him for battle in book 18 of the *Iliad*. Ma Joad forces her gift of seven dollars on Tom to help on his perilous way. Full of his new mission in life, he does not respond to the love his mother expresses for him, but simply says, "Good-by." Ma returns to the camp, and Tom presumably will go on to his doom as Casy did before him but also to a sort of immortality for men who have fought for social justice:

> "Then I'll be all aroun' in the dark. I'll be ever'where—wherever you look. Wherever they's a fight so hungry people can eat, I'll be there. Wherever they's a cop beatin' up a guy, I'll be there. If Casy knowed, why, I'll be in the way guys yell when they're mad an'—I'll be in the way kids laugh when they're hungry an' they know supper's ready. An' when our folks eat the stuff they raise an' live in the houses they build—why, I'll be there." (P. 572)

This is a kind of immortality that Ma "don' un'erstan'," although it is she who confers it on him by making his heroism possible.

It is not enough to say that this wonderful scene is inspired by the New Testament story of Christ's resurrection from the tomb.[5] The "caves of vines" and the tomb are the womb from which the hero is delivered to a new life, but the landscape in Steinbeck's scene is more nearly that of the classical underworld. The nourishing of the hero-son by the earth-goddess mother until he is

[5]See H. Kelly Crockett, "The Bible and *The Grapes of Wrath*," *College English*, 24 (December 1962), 197; Charles C. Dougherty, "The Christ Figure in *The Grapes of Wrath*," ibid., p. 226.

strong enough to leave her suggests the myth of Ishtar and Tammuz, and the commitment of the son of war and eventual death recalls the sad exchange between Thetis and Achilles. Tom Joad's "death" brings an end to his ordinary existence as one of thousands of Okies; he is reborn into the life of the epic hero, who dooms himself to an early death as soon as he elects a heroic course of action. His consecration is affirmed by his discipleship to Casy and the ritual release performed by his mother. If there is a resurrection, it is the resurrection of Casy in Tom. Tom's rebirth through the agency of Casy and Ma Joad has a striking antecedent in the experience of Henry Fleming in Crane's *Red Badge of Courage.* The change in Henry's attitude toward heroism—from callow sentimentality to a mature sense of its real consequences—is in part wrought by the example of Jim Conklin, another Christ-like figure, and Henry's encounter with death in the forest, alone, and rebirth among his comrades.[6]

The rebirth of Tom as hero is emphasized by the ironical implication of another incident. Shortly after Ma Joad has returned from the stream and the willows, the pregnant Rosasharn distractedly seeks refuge in the very same place, along "the stream and the trail that went beside it." She lies down among the berry vines and feels "the weight of the baby inside her." Not long after this the rains come. Pa Joad and other men in the camp work feverishly to hold back the swollen stream from flooding their miserable living quarters; they build an earth embankment, but it is swept away and the water washes into the camp. At the same time Ma Joad and some neighboring women are helping Rosasharn deliver her baby, but they meet with no greater success—the baby is stillborn. Uncle John is delegated to bury the "blue shriveled little mummy"; instead, he takes the apple box it is in and floats it down the river, hoping that it will be a sign to the California landowners of the Okies' sore affliction. "Go down an' tell 'em," he says, in words echoing the Negro spiritual "Go Down, Moses" and thus linking three oppressed peoples—Israelites, American Negro slaves, and the Okies. The river is the same that saw the rebirth of Tom, who is a kind of Moses to his people, and now it receives the dead infant.

[6]See John E. Hart, *"The Red Badge of Courage* as Myth and Symbol," *University of Kansas City Review*, 19 (Summer 1953), 249–56.

In Tom the Biblical and epic traditions of the hero came together to make a proletarian leader of the twentieth century. The man of anger and the quick blow of revenge is also the disciple devoted to self-sacrifice in the cause of the downtrodden and deprived. The son of the spouse-goddess is released from the death that is the family in order to do battle for the class that will possess the future. The man of violence bred from personal pride—Tom killed his first man in a tavern brawl—is baptized in the violence of class struggle, and he turns, like the classical hero, from the defense of his own rights to the defense of all men's rights. Like Presley in *The Octopus,* Tom is an apprentice-hero who learns from a man more experienced in warfare, in class warfare. What Presley learns from his mentor, the anarchist barkeep, is in the same political tradition as what Tom learns from Casy; the leftist attack on capitalism is rejected by Norris, however, and seemingly accepted by Steinbeck after it is filtered through Christian feeling and presented in Biblical and epic images.

The Grapes of Wrath begins with a drought bringing death to the land and dispossession to its inhabitants and ends ironically with a flood that again destroys the land and disperses the people. Nature as well as society dooms the Okies, who fall from one catastrophe into another, losing their land, their belongings, their livelihood, and finally even their miserable shelters. But in spite of homelessness and despair, the Joads have succeeded in making an important journey, passing from one bond, the family, to another, mankind. "They's changes—all over," it is said. "Use' ta be the fambly was fust. It ain't so now. It's anybody." In place of the family a new form of social organization is tentatively envisaged on the model of a small socialist community. Not all can see the promised land—only Casy, who does not live to enter it, and Tom, who is on the verge of entering it at the close of the book. Pa Joad's symbolical attempt, in fighting the river, to unite the community after the old style of neighborly cooperation comes too late and fails. Having long since relinquished control of the family to Ma, Pa Joad is a man without a role to play in the world. He joins Magnus Derrick in the company of those in the older generation who, unable to accommodate themselves to a new situation, are only pitifully heroic. Others, those who seek individual solutions, are shown to be equally futile. Muley Graves stays on the abandoned farmlands in Oklahoma and must live "like a coyote" on the trash left behind and the wild animals still surviving on the plains. Uncle Noah wanders away down a river he half-wittedly fancies, and Uncle John gets drunk when he can sneak the money. Al, Tom's younger brother, strikes out for himself, ironically to start another hapless family. While Ma cannot understand Tom's social idealism, she and Rosasharn do come around to the side of humanity in the closing scene of the book when Rosasharn, with her mother's prompting, feeds to a dying old man, a stranger, the milk her body had stored for her child. With neither child nor husband Rosasharn must abandon the idea of family. Ma's family has disintegrated, Rosasharn's has not even had a chance to begin.

The images of the community and the hero that dominate the ending of *The Grapes of Wrath* are pitiful enough: a fugitive coming out of hiding to do unequal battle with an infinitely superior enemy and two frightened women trying desperately to save a dying old man in an empty barn. It seems to be an image of miserable survival in the face of awesome odds. Still, out of the sordid circumstances of a purely naturalistic life a hero is born in a manner reminiscent of great heroes of the past. The affirmation of a better future seems groundless, but there is affirmation nonetheless, and a hero is ready to attempt its achievement by leading people who have prepared themselves for a new kind of society. "The book is neither riddle nor tragedy," insists Warren French, "it is an epic comedy of the triumph of the 'holy spirit.' "[7]

Norris explores the possibilities of heroism in one novel, Steinbeck and Hemingway in a whole succession of novels. Steinbeck seems to want to believe in heroic behavior and the ideal community, yet in one novel after another he submits a negative report as to the chances of either in our time. His first novel, *Cup of Gold* (1929), in Warren French's summary, "asserts that there is no place for the swashbuckling hero in the modern world."[8] In *Tortilla Flat* (1935) Steinbeck lovingly presents the irregular habits and amusing antics of a number of paisanos, but at the same time, by stressing a mock-heroic parallel with Malory's *Morte d'Arthur,* he insists upon our viewing their attempts to be heroic as ridiculous. In the end, Danny, the Arthur of a paisano Round Table, armed

[7]*John Steinbeck* (New York, 1961), p. 107.
[8]Ibid., p. 37.

with a broken table leg, goes out to do battle and dies in a duel with "The Enemy" in the "gulch," a place which he and his companions used for want of an outhouse. Although the hero in the next novel, *In Dubious Battle* (1936), bears a slight resemblance to another figure from the Arthurian legend, Percival, the mood of this work is starkly naturalistic. Jim Nolan's attempt to become the leader of embattled laborers is soon ended by the blast of a shotgun that renders him, horribly and quite literally, a hero without a face. His epitaph is spoken by his mentor, Mac, and is necessarily brief: "Comrades! He didn't want nothing for himself—." Lennie, the hero in *Of Mice and Men* (1937), is a feebleminded giant, "shapeless of face," and obviously incapable of responsible behavior. In his time of trouble he takes refuge in a place near a river where a path winds "through the willows and among the sycamores." But Lennie is not reborn there; his best friend must become his executioner there because Lennie cannot control the great strength he has and is consequently a menace to the community.

In *The Grapes of Wrath*, for the first time, Steinbeck offers a not altogether forlorn image of the epic hero. Tom Joad is a hero with a face, badly battered though it is; he survives the assault upon him, his spirit is revived at a place where willows grow by a stream and, presumably, he is embarked upon a heroic career. Jim Nolan finishes before he ever really begins, and the possibility of rebirth never materializes. Just before his death Mac advises him of a place of refuge should the occasion ever arise, "a deep cave" hidden by willows near a stream. But Jim never gets to the cave; he dies actually, not symbolically as Tom does. Nor does Jim have Ma Joad as his protective goddess and Casy as his martyred mentor. Mac, a hardheaded and cautious labor organizer, does not have the mythical credentials to inspire a hero. Lennie also has a cave to retire to if he becomes too much of a burden to his friend George, but there is no returning from it. Only Tom returns from the cave and the willows, the place of death, to present the face of a hero to the world, a face so badly scarred that he can no longer be recognized as Tom Joad. Of all Steinbeck's heroes, he is the only one who affirms the possibility of a hero arising out of the anonymity of twentieth-century economic strife and still bearing the signs of an ancient dedication.

PART TWO
Viewpoints

The Grapes of Wrath

by George Bluestone

In his compact little study of California writers, *The Boys in the Back Room,* Edmund Wilson comments on the problems inherent in the close affiliation between Hollywood and commercial fiction:

> ... Since the people who control the movies will not go a step of the way to give the script-writer a chance to do a serious script, the novelist seems, consciously or unconsciously, to be going part of the way to meet the producers. John Steinbeck, in *The Grapes of Wrath*, has certainly learned from the films—and not only from such documentary pictures of Pare Lorentz, but from the sentimental symbolism of Hollywood. The result is that *The Grapes of Wrath* has poured itself on to the screen as easily as if it had been written in the studios, and that it is probably the sole serious story on record that seems almost equally effective as a book and as a film. . . .[1]

Indeed, not only did Steinbeck learn from Pare Lorentz; he also received, through Lorentz, his first introduction to Nunnally Johnson, the screen writer who did the movie adaptation of his novel.[2] And Bennett Cerf, the publishing head of Random House, must have had none other than Steinbeck in mind when he wrote, "The thing an author wants most from his publisher these days is a letter of introduction to Darryl Zanuck."[3] For if Steinbeck was fortunate in having Pare Lorentz as a teacher and Nunnally Johnson as a screen writer, he was one of the few who earned the coveted letter to Darryl Zanuck, the producer of *The Grapes of*

"The Grapes of Wrath." From *Novels into Film* by George Bluestone (Baltimore: The Johns Hopkins Press, 1957), pp. 147–69. Copyright 1957 by the Johns Hopkins Press. Reprinted by permission of the publisher.

[1]Edmund Wilson, *Classics and Commercials: A Literary Chronicle of the Forties* (New York: Farrar, Straus and Co., 1950), p. 49.

[2]In conversation with Mr. Johnson.

[3]In *Hollywood Reporter* (January 9, 1941), p. 3; quoted in Leo C. Rosten, *Hollywood: The Movie Colony, The Movie Makers* (New York, 1941), p. 366.

Wrath. Add Gregg Toland's photography, Alfred Newman's music, and John Ford's direction, and one sees that Steinbeck had an unusually talented crew, one which could be depended upon to respect the integrity of his best-selling book.

Lester Asheim, in his close charting of the correspondence between twenty-four novels and films, seems to corroborate Edmund Wilson's conclusion about the easy transference of Steinbeck's book to John Ford's film. According to Asheim's analysis, the major sequences in the novel bear more or less the same ratio to the whole as the corresponding sequences do in the film:

	percent of whole	
sequence	*book*	*film*
Oklahoma episodes	20	28
Cross-country episodes	19	22
General commentary	17	—
Government camp episodes	15	18
Hooverville episodes	10	13
Strike-breaking episodes	9	16
Final episodes	10	3
	100	100

And when Asheim goes on to explain that, if one ignores the major deletions which occur in the transference and considers only those episodes in the novel which appear in the film, the percentage of both book and film devoted to these central events would be virtually identical, his observation seems, at first, to be providing indisputable proof for Wilson's claim.[4]

Yet, to follow through Wilson's primary analysis of Steinbeck's work is to come at once on a contradiction which belies, first, his comment on the ineluctable fitness of the novel for Hollywood consumption and, second, his implication that Steinbeck, like the novelists whom Bennett Cerf has in mind, had written with one eye on the movie market. For it is central to Wilson's critical argument that the "substratum which remains constant" in Steinbeck's work "is his preoccupation with biology."[5] According to Wilson's view, "Mr. Steinbeck almost always in his fiction is dealing either with the lower animals or with human beings so

---

[4]Lester Asheim, "From Book to Film" (Ph.D. dissertation, University of Chicago, 1949), pp. 55–56.
[5]Wilson, p. 42.

rudimentary that they are almost on the animal level."[6] Tracing the thematic seams that run through Steinbeck's prose, Wilson notes the familiar interchapter on the turtle whose slow, tough progress survives the gratuitous cruelty of the truck driver who swerves to hit it. This anticipates the survival of the Joads, who, with the same dorsal hardness, will manage another journey along a road, emerging like the turtle from incredible hardships surrounded by symbols of fertility, much like the turtle's "wild cat head" which spawns three spearhead seeds in the dry ground. And Wilson notes, too, the way in which the forced pilgrimage of the Joads, adumbrated by the turtle's indestructibility, is "accompanied and parodied all the way by animals, insects and birds," as when the abandoned house where Tom finds Muley is invaded by bats, weasels, owls, mice, and pet cats gone wild.

This primary biological analysis seems to contradict Wilson's more casual statement on the film, since the screen version, as evolved by Nunnally Johnson and John Ford, contains little evidence of this sort of preoccupation. And when Asheim concludes, after a detailed comparison, that to one unfamiliar with the novel there are no loose ends or glaring contradictions to indicate that alterations have taken place,[7] we begin to uncover a series of disparities which, rather than demonstrating the ease of adaptation, suggests its peculiar difficulties. We are presented in the film with what Asheim calls "a new logic of events," a logic which deviates from the novel in several important respects. Tracing these mutations in some detail will illuminate the special characteristics of book and film alike. The question immediately arises, how could *The Grapes of Wrath* have gone on the screen so easily when the biological emphasis is nowhere present?

Undeniably, there is, in the novel, a concurrence of animal and human life similar to that which appears in the work of Walter Van Tilburg Clark, another western writer who transcends regional themes. Even from the opening of the chapter which depicts the pedestrian endurance of the turtle, creature and human are linked:

> The concrete highway was edged with a mat of tangled, broken, dry grass, and the grass heads were heavy with oat beards to catch on a dog's coat, and foxtails to tangle in a horse's fetlocks, and clover

[6]*Ibid.*, pp. 42–43.
[7]Asheim, p. 161.

burrs to fasten in a sheep's wool; sleeping life waiting to be spread and dispersed, every seed armed with an appliance of dispersal, twisting darts and parachutes for the wind, little spears and balls of tiny thorns, and all waiting for animals and for the wind, for a man's trouser cuff or the hem of a woman's skirt, all passive but armed appliances of activity, still, but each possessed of the anlage of movement.

Here, the central motifs of the narrative are carefully, but inobtrusively enunciated, a kind of generalized analogue to the coming tribulations of the Joads: a harsh, natural order which is distracting to men and dogs alike; a hostile, dry passivity which, like the dormant blastema, is at the same time laden with regenerative possibilities. From the opening passages ("Gophers and ant lions started small avalanches . . .") to the last scene in which an attempt is made to beatify Rose of Sharon's biological act, the narrative is richly interspersed with literal and figurative zoology. Tom and Casy witness the unsuccessful efforts of a cat to stop the turtle's slow progress. In the deserted house, Muley describes himself as having once been "mean like a wolf," whereas now he is "mean like a weasel." Ma Joad describes the law's pursuit of Pretty Boy Floyd in animal terms: "they run him like a coyote, an' him a-snappin' an' a-snarlin', mean as a lobo." Young Al boasts that his Hudson jalopy will "ride like a bull calf." In the interchapter describing the change, the growing wrath triggered by the wholesale evictions of the tenant farmers, the western states are "nervous as horses before a thunder storm."

Later, Ma Joad savagely protests the break-up of the family: "All we got is the family unbroke. Like a bunch of cows, when the lobos are ranging." Later still, Tom tells Casy that the day he got out of prison, he ran himself down a prostitute "like she was a rabbit." Even the endless caravans of jalopies are described in terms which echo the plodding endurance of the turtle. After a night in which "the owls coasted overhead, and the coyotes gabbled in the distance, and into the camp skunks walked, looking for bits of food . . ." the morning comes, revealing the cars of migrants along the highway crawling out "like bugs." After the relatively peaceful interlude of the Government Camp, Al comments on the practice of periodically burning out the Hoovervilles where the dispossessed farmers are forced to cluster: ". . . they jus' go hide down in the willows an' then they come out an' build 'em another weed shack. Jus' like gophers." And finally, toward the end, Ma expresses her longing to have a settled home for Ruth and Winfield, the youngest children, in order to keep them from becoming wild animals. For by this time, Ruth and Winnie do, indeed, emerge from their beds "like hermit crabs from shells."

The persistence of this imagery reveals at least part of its service. In the first place, even in our random selections, biology supports and comments upon sociology. Sexual activity, the primacy of the family clan, the threat and utility of industrial machinery, the alienation and hostility of the law, the growing anger at economic oppression, the arguments for human dignity, are all accompanied by, or expressed in terms of, zoological images. In the second place, the presence of literal and figurative animals is more frequent when the oppression of the Joads is most severe. The pattern of the novel, as we shall see, is similar to a parabola whose highest point is the sequence at the Government Camp. From Chapter XXII to the middle of Chapter XXVI, which covers this interlude, the animal imagery is almost totally absent. Densely compacted at the beginning, when Tom returns to find his home a shambles, it recurs in the closing sequences of the strike-breaking and the flood.

The point is that none of this appears in the film. Even the highly cinematic passage depicting the slaughtering of the pigs, in preparation for the journey, is nowhere evident in the final editing. If the film adaptation remains at all faithful to its original, it is not in retaining what Edmund Wilson calls the constant substratum in Steinbeck's work. It is true, one may argue, that biological functions survive in the Joads' elementary fight for life, in the animal preoccupation with finding food and shelter, in the scenes of death and procreation, but this is not what Edmund Wilson has in mind. In the film, these functions are interwoven so closely with a number of other themes that in no sense can the biological preoccupation be said to have a primary value. This type of deletion could not have been arbitrary, for, as Vachel Lindsay showed as early as 1915, animal imagery can be used quite effectively as cinema. Reviewing Griffith's *The Avenging Conscience,* Lindsay is describing the meditations of a boy who has just been forced to say goodbye to his beloved, supposedly forever. Watching a spider in his web devour a fly, the boy meditates on the cruelty of nature: "Then he sees the ants in turn destroy the spider. The pictures are shown on so large a scale that the spiderweb fills the end of the theater. Then the ant-tragedy does the same. They can be classed as particularly apt hieroglyphics. . . ."[8] More recently, the killing of the animals by the boy in *Les Jeux Interdits* shows that biology can still effectively support cinematic themes. In the particular case of *The Grapes of Wrath*, however, the suggestions of the book were abandoned. If, then, we are to understand the mutation, to assess the film's special achievement, we must look elsewhere.

Immediately, a number of other motifs strongly assert themselves in Steinbeck's novel: the juxtaposition of natural morality and religious hypocrisy; the love of the regenerative land; the primacy of the family; the dignity of human beings; the sociopolitical implications inherent in the conflict between individual work and industrial oppression. Consider Casy's impulsive rationalizations in the very early section of the book where he tries, like the Ancient Mariner, to convince his listener and himself at the same time, that his rejection of religious preaching in favor of a kind of naturalistic code of ethics is morally acceptable. Tortured by his sexual impulses as a preacher, Casy began to doubt and question the assumptions which he had been articulating from his rough, evangelical pulpit, began to observe the discrepancy between theoretical sin and factual behavior. He repeats his conclusions to Tom, "Maybe it ain't a sin. Maybe it's just the way folks is. Maybe we been whippin' hell out of ourselves for nothin'. . . . To hell with it! There ain't no sin and there ain't no virtue. There's just stuff people do. It's all part of the same thing. And some of the things folks do is nice, and some ain't nice, but that's as far as any man got a right to say."

Casy retains his love for people, but not through his ministry, and later this love will be transmuted into personal sacrifice and the solidarity of union organization. This suspicion of a theology not rooted in ordinary human needs continues to echo throughout the novel. When Casy refuses to pray for the dying Grampa, Granma reminds him, quite offhandedly, how Ruthie prayed when she was a little girl: " 'Now I lay me down to sleep. I pray the Lord my soul to keep. An' when she got there the cupboard was bare, an' so the poor dog got none.' " The moral is clear: in the face of hunger, religious piety seems absurd. After Grampa's death, the inclusion of a line from Scripture in the note that will follow him to his grave is parodied in much the same way, but Casy's last words at the grave echo his earlier statement: "This here

---

[8]Vachel Lindsay, *The Art of the Moving Picture* (New York, 1915), p. 124.

ol' man jus' lived a life an' jus' died out of it. I don't know whether he was good or bad, but that don't matter much. He was alive, an' that's what matters. An' now he's dead, an' that don't matter. . . . if I was to pray, it'd be for the folks that don' know which way to turn." Ma Joad expresses the same kind of mystical acceptance of the life cycle when she tries to tell Rose of Sharon about the hurt of childbearing:

> They's a time of change, an' when that comes, dyin' is a piece of all dyin', and bearin' is a piece of all bearin', and bearin' an' dyin' is two pieces of the same thing. An' then things ain't lonely any more. An' then a hurt don't hurt so bad, 'cause it ain't a lonely hurt no more, Rose-asharn. I wisht I could tell you so you'd know, but I can't.

Because Ma is so firm in her belief in the rightness of natural processes, she becomes furious at the religious hypocrites who plague the migrants. At the Hoovervilles and in the government station, the evangelists whom Ma characterizes as Holy Rollers and Jehovites are grimly present, like camp followers. Beginning with polite acceptance, Ma becomes infuriated when one of these zealots works on Rose of Sharon, scaring her half to death with visions of hellfire and burning. Ma represents the state of natural grace to which Casy aspires from the beginning.

Just as the novel reveals a preoccupation with biology, it is also obsessed with love of the earth. From the opening lines of the book, "To the red country and part of the gray country of Oklahoma, the last rains came gently, and they did not cut the scarred earth," to the last scene of desolation, the land imagery persists. The earth motif is woven into the texture complexly, but on the whole it serves two main functions: first, to signify love; and second, to signify endurance. Tom makes the sexual connection when, listening to Casy's compulsive story, he idly, but quite naturally, draws the torso of a woman in the dirt, "breasts, hips, pelvis." The attachment of the men for the land is often so intense that it borders on sexual love. Muley's refusal to leave, even after the caterpillar tractors have wiped him out, looks ahead to Grampa's similar recalcitrance. At first, Grampa is enthusiastic about the prospect of moving to a more fertile land, and he delivers himself of words verging on panegyric: "Jus' let me get out to California where I can pick me an orange when I want it. Or grapes. There's a thing I ain't ever had enough of. Gonna get me a whole big bunch a grapes off a bush, or whatever, an' I'm gonna squash 'em on my face, an' let 'em run offen my chin." But when the moment for departures arrives, Grampa refuses to go. His roots in the ground are too strong; he cannot bear to tear them up. Very soon after the family leaves its native soil, Grampa dies of a stroke. And when Casy says to Noah, "Grampa an' the old place, they was jus' the same thing," we feel that the observation has a precision which is supported by the texture of the entire novel. When the Joads get to California, they will, of course, find that the grapes which Grampa dreamed of are inaccessible, that the grapes of promise inevitably turn to grapes of wrath. The land, one interchapter tells, has been possessed by the men with a frantic hunger for land who came before the Joads. And the defeated promise is bitterly dramatized in the last scene, when a geranium, the last flower of earth to appear in the novel, becomes an issue dividing Ruthie and Winfield, and results in Ruthie's pressing one petal against Winfield's nose, cruelly. Love and endurance have been tried to their utmost. When the land goes, everything else goes, too; and the water is the emblem of its destruction.

Love of family parallels love of the earth. During the threatening instability of the cross-country journey, Ma Joad acts as the cohesive force which keeps her brood intact. Whenever one of the men threatens to leave, Ma protests, and sometimes savagely. When she takes over leadership of the family, by defying Pa Joad with a jack handle, it is over the question of whether or not Tom shall stay behind with the disabled car. Even after Connie, Rose of Sharon's husband, and Noah, one of the brothers, desert the family, the identity of the clan remains Ma Joad's primary fixation. After half a continent of hardship, Ma articulates her deepest feelings. She tells Tom, "They was a time when we was on the lan'. They was a boundary to us then. Ol' folks died off, an' little fellas came, an' we was always one thing—we was the fambly—kinda whole and clear. An' now we ain't clear no more." The deprivation of the native land, and the alienation of the new, become more than economic disasters; they threaten the only social organization upon which Ma Joad can depend. The fertility of the land and the integrity of the clan are no longer distinct entities; both are essential for survival.

Closely bound up with this theme of familial survival is the theme of human dignity. Clearly, the exigencies of eviction and migration force the problem of brute survival upon the Joads. But just as important is the correlative theme of human dignity. The first time the Joads are addressed as "Okies," by a loud-mouthed deputy who sports a Sam Browne belt and pistol holster, Ma is so shocked that she almost attacks him. Later, Uncle John is so chagrined by Casy's sacrificial act (deflecting from Tom the blame for hitting the deputy, and going to prison in his stead) that he feels positively sinful for not making an equal contribution. At the Government Camp, a woman complains about taking charity from the Salvation Army because "We was hungry—they made us crawl for our dinner. They took our dignity." But it is Tom who makes the most articulate defense of dignity against the legal harassment to which the Joads have been subjected: ". . . if it was the law they was workin' with, why, we could take it. But it *ain't* the law. They're a-workin' away at our spirits. . . . They're workin' on our decency." And the final image of Rose of Sharon offering her breast to the starving farmer is intended as an apotheosis of the scared girl, recently deprived of her child, into a kind of natural madonna.

In short, if the biological interest exists, it is so chastened through suffering that it achieves a dignity which is anything but animal, in Edmund Wilson's sense of the word. The conflicts, values, and recognitions of the Joads cannot, therefore, be equated with the preoccupations of subhuman life. The biological life may be retained in the search for food and shelter, in the cycle of death and procreation, but always in terms which emphasize rather than obliterate the distinctions between humans and animals. When Steinbeck reminisces about his carefree bohemian days in Monterey, he is just as nostalgic about the freedom of assorted drifters, his "interesting and improbable" characters, as he is about Ed Ricketts' "commercial biological laboratory."[9] Steinbeck's novel may be read, then, as much as a flight from biological determinism as a representation of it. The story of the pilgrimage to the new Canaan which is California, the cycle of death and birth through which the Joads must suffer, becomes a moral, as well as a physical, trial by fire.

The socio-political implications of the Joad story, more familiar than these correlative themes, serve to counterpoint and define the anger and the suffering. Throughout the novel, the Joads are haunted by deputies in the service of landowners, bankers, and

---

[9]John Steinbeck, "Dreams Piped from Cannery Row," *New York Times Theater Section* (Sunday, November 27, 1955), p. 1.

fruit growers; by the contradiction between endless acres in full harvest and streams of migratory workers in dire straits; by un-scrupulous businessmen who take advantage of the desperate, westbound caravans; by strikebreakers, corrupt politicians, and thugs. At first, the Joads must draw from their meager savings to pay for gas and half-loaves of bread; but as they draw West they must even pay for water. In California, they cannot vote, are kept continually on the move, are bullied by the constabulary, and must even watch helplessly as one of the Hoovervilles is burned out. The only time they earn enough money to eat comes when they are hired as strike breakers. Gradually, there is the dawning recognition that the only possible response to these impossible conditions is solidarity through union organization, precisely what the fruit growers and their agents dread most. In order to overcome the fruit growers' divisive tactics, Casy becomes an active union organizer and gets killed in the process by a bunch of marauding deputies. At the end, Tom, in his familiar farewell to Ma Joad, is trembling on the verge of Casy's solution. "That the end will be revolution," one reviewer writes, "is implicit from the title onwards."[10] Steinbeck ultimately withdraws from such a didactic conclusion, as we shall see in a moment, but that the didactic conclusion is implicit in the narrative can hardly be denied:

> . . . the companies, the banks worked at their own doom and they did not know it. The fields were fruitful, and starving men moved on the roads. The granaries were full and the children of the poor grew up rachitic, and the pustules of pellagra swelled on their sides. The great companies did not know that the line between hunger and anger is a thin line. And money that might have gone to wages went for gas, for guns, for agents and spies, for blacklists, for drilling. On the highways the people moved like ants and searched for work, for food. And the anger began to ferment.

Hence the symbolism of the title. Clearly woven through the novel, and therefore inseparable from Steinbeck's prose, we find these sharp political overtones. Besides being a novel, writes one reviewer, *The Grapes of Wrath* "is a monograph on rural sociology, a manual of practical wisdom in times of enormous stress, an assault on individualism, an essay in behalf of a rather vague form of pan-theism, and a bitter, ironical attack on that emotional evangelistic

[10]Earle Birney, "The Grapes of Wrath," *Canadian Forum*, XIX (June 1939), 95.

religion which seems to thrive in the more impoverished rural districts of this vast country. . . ."[11]

Along the highways, a new social order is improvised, a fluid but permanent council in which the family is the basic unit, an order reaching its almost utopian operation at the Government Camp. According to this scheme, the governing laws remain constant, while the specific counters are continually replaced, one family succeeding another, a sort of permanent republic which can accommodate a populace in constant motion:

> The families learned what rights must be observed—the right of privacy in the tent; the right to keep the past black hidden in the heart; the right to talk and to listen; the right to refuse help or to decline it; the right of son to court and daughter to be courted; the right of the hungry to be fed; the rights of the pregnant and the sick to transcend all other rights. . . .
>
> And with the laws, the punishments—and there were only two— a quick and murderous fight or ostracism; and ostracism was the worst.

Within such a scheme, Ma Joad's fierce maintenance of the family becomes more clear. For without the integrity of the clan, survival is all but impossible. The alternatives are death, which does, in fact, snip the Joad family at both ends, claiming both the grandparents and Rose of Sharon's baby, or, on the other hand, militant struggle through union organization.

If the biological motifs do not appear in the film, these correlative themes are adopted with varying degrees of emphasis. The religious satire, with a single exception, is dropped entirely; the political radicalism is muted and generalized; but the insistence on family cohesion, on affinity for the land, on human dignity is carried over into the movie version.

In the film, the one remnant of tragi-comic religious satire occurs in Tom's first talk with Casy on the way to the Joad house. Casy's probing self-analysis is essentially the same as in the book, and its culmination, "There ain't no sin an' there ain't no virtue. There's just what people do," is a precise copy from the novel. Once the theme is enunciated, however, it is underplayed, recurring almost imperceptibly in the burial scene. Ma's anger at the evangelical camp followers is dropped entirely.

[11]James N. Vaughan, "The Grapes of Wrath," *Commonweal*, XXX (July 28, 1949), 341–342.

The film-makers must have known that the film was political dynamite. After a difficult decision, Darryl Zanuck began what turned out to be, thematically speaking, one of the boldest films in the history of the movies. The secrecy which surrounded the studios during production has become legend. Even as the film was being shot, Zanuck reportedly received 15,000 letters, 99 per cent of which accused him of cowardice, saying he would never make the film because the industry was too closely associated with big business.[12] And yet, fearful that the Texas and Oklahoma Chambers of Commerce would object to the shooting, on their territory, of the *enfant terrible* of the publishing world, the studio announced that it was really filming another story innocuously entitled, *Highway 66.*[13] It was precisely this fear of criticism, of giving offense to vested interests that was responsible for muting the film's political implications. Lester Asheim has pointed out how the film scrupulously steers clear of the book's specific accusations. Many small episodes showing unfair business practices, for example, were cut from the film version.[14] While the reference to the handbills which flood Oklahoma, luring an excess labor force out West, is carried over into the film, most of the corresponding details are dropped. The complaint about the unfair practices of used-car salesmen; the argument with the camp owner about overcharging; the depiction of the company-store credit racket; the dishonest scales on the fruit ranch; and even the practice, on the part of an otherwise sympathetic luncheon proprietor, of taking the jackpots from his own slot machines—none of these was ever even proposed for the shooting-script. Similarly, all legal authority is carefully exempt from blame. In Tom's angry speech about the indignities foisted upon the family by the local constabulary, everything is retained except his bitter indictment of the deputies, and his line, ". . . they comes a time when the on'y way a fella can keep his decency is by takin' a sock at a cop."[15] In Casy's discourse on the progress of the fruit strike, the line, "An' all the cops in the worl' come down on us" is deleted. Casy's announcement that the cops have threatened to beat up recalcitrant strikers is retained, but the film adds, "Not them reg'lar deputies, but them tin badge fellas they call guards. . . ."

[12]Frank Condon, "The Grapes of Raps," *Collier's* (January 27, 1940), p. 67.
[13]*Ibid.,* p. 64.
[14]Asheim, p. 277.
[15]*Ibid.,* p. 256.

In spite of the revolutionary candor of the interchapters, whenever the film raises questions about whom to see or what to do for recourse or complaint, the novel's evasive answers are used in reply. When Tom asks the proprietor of the Government Camp why there aren't more places like this, the proprietor answers, "You'll have to find that out for yourself." When Muley wants to find out from the City Man who's to blame for his eviction, so that he can take a shotgun to him, the City Man tells him that the Shawnee Land and Cattle Company is so amorphous that it cannot be properly located. The bank in Tulsa is responsible for telling the land company what to do, but the bank's manager is simply an employee trying to keep up with orders from the East. "Then who do we shoot?" Muley asks in exasperation. "Brother, I don't know . . ." the City Man answers helplessly. To add to the mystification, the film supplies a few clouds of its own. In the scene where Farmer Thomas warns Tom and the Wallaces about the impending raid on the Government Camp, the recurring question of "red" agitation comes up again. The "red menace" has become the *raison d'être* for attacks against the squatter camps. Tom, who has heard the argument before, bursts out, "What is these reds anyway?" Originally, according to the script, Wilkie Wallace was to have answered, cribbing his own line from the novel, that according to a fruit grower he knew once, a red is anyone who "wants thirty-cents an hour when I'm payin' twenty-five." In the final print, however, Farmer Thomas answers Tom's question simply but evasively, "I ain't talkin' about that one way 'r another," and goes on to warn the men about the raid.

Even Tom's much-quoted farewell to Ma Joad, retained in the film, is pruned until little remains but its mystical affirmation. And the final words, backing away from Casy's conscious social commitment, are carried over intact:

Ma. I don' un'erstan. . . .
Tom. Me neither, Ma. . . . It's jus' stuff I been thinkin' about. . . .

In the world of the Ford-Johnson film, the politico-economic tendency is merely an urge in search of a name it is never allowed to find. And yet because of the naked suffering, the brute struggle to survive, devoid of solutions in either church or revolution, John Gassner finds that more appropriate than the image of God "trampling out the vintage where the grapes of wrath are stored," from which the title is derived, are the lines, "And here in dust and dirt ... the lilies of his love appear,"[16] which connote neither religion nor politics. According to Gassner, bed-rock is reached in this film, "and it proves to be as hard as granite and as soft as down."

If the religious satire is absent and the politics muted, the love of land, family and human dignity are consistently translated into effective cinematic images. Behind the director's controlling hand is the documentary eye of a Pare Lorentz or a Robert Flaherty, of the vision in those stills produced by the Resettlement Administration in its volume, *Land of the Free* (with commentary by Archibald MacLeish), or in Walker Evans' shots for *Let Us Now Praise Famous Men* (with commentary by James Agee), which, like Lorentz's work, was carried on under the auspices of the Farm Security Administration. Gregg Toland's photography is acutely conscious of the pictorial values of land and sky, finding equivalents for those haunting images of erosion which were popularized for the New Deal's reclamation program and reflected in Steinbeck's prose. The constant use of brooding, dark silhouettes against light, translucent skies, the shots of roads and farms, the fidelity to the speech, manners and dress of Oklahoma farmers—all contribute to the pictorial mood and tone. I am told that some of these exteriors were shot on indoor sound stages at the studio,[17] but even this has worked to the advantage of the film-makers. In the studio, Ford was able to control his composition by precise lighting, so that some of the visuals—Tom moving like an ant against a sky bright with luminous clouds, the caravans of jalopies, the slow rise of the dust storm—combine physical reality with careful composition to create striking pictorial effects. Finally, generous selections of dialogue, culled from the novel, echoing the theme of family affiliation with the land, appear in the final movie version. Grampa's last minute refusal to go, as he clutches at a handful of soil, necessitates Tom's plan to get him drunk and carry him aboard by force. And, as Muley, John Qualen's apostrophe to the land, after the tractor has ploughed into his shack, is one of the most poignant anywhere in films.

In the same fashion, the central episodes depicting Ma Joad's insistence on family cohesion, and Tom's insistence on dignity, are either presented directly or clearly suggested. Ma, to be sure, is made a little less fierce than she is in the novel. Tom still tells Casy

[16]John Gassner, *Twenty Best Film Plays,* ed. John Gassner and Dudley Nichols (New York, 1943), p. xxvi.
[17]In an interview with Mr. Ford.

the anecdote about Ma's taking after a tin peddler with an ax in one hand and a chicken in the other, but the scene in which she takes a jack handle after Pa, originally scheduled according to the script, is deleted. We never see Ma physically violent.

Tracing through these recurring themes, comparing and contrasting the emphasis given to each, gives us all the advantages of content analysis without explaining, finally, the central difference between Steinbeck's artistic vision and that of the film-makers. This difference does emerge, however, when we compare the two structures.

Some deletions, additions, and alterations, to be sure, reflect in a general way the ordinary process of mutation from a linguistic to a visual medium. On the one hand, the characteristic interchapters in the novel are dropped entirely, those interludes which adopt the author's point of view and which are at once more lyric and less realistic than the rest of the prose. The angry interludes, the explicit indictments, the authorial commentary do not appear, indeed would seem obtrusive, in the film. Translated into observed reality, however, and integrated into the picture within the frame, certain fragments find their proper filmic equivalents. For example, the interchapters are mined for significant dialogue, and, in fact, Muley's moving lines, "We were born on it, and we got killed on it, died on it. Even if it's no good, it's still ours. . . ." appear originally in one of these interludes. In the second place, the themes of one or two of these interchapters are translated into a few highly effective montages—the coming of the tractors, the caravans of jalopies, the highway signs along Route 66. As Muley begins telling his story, over the candle in the dimly lit cabin, the film flashes back to the actual scene. A series of tractors looming up like mechanical creatures over the horizon, crossing and crisscrossing the furrowed land, cuts to the one tractor driven by the Davis boy, who has been assigned the task of clearing off Muley's farm. Later, as the Joads' jalopy begins its pilgrimage, we see a similar shot of scores and scores of other jalopies, superimposed one upon the other, making the same, slow, desperate crosscountry trek. Finally, the central episodes of the trip are bridged by montages of road signs—"Checotah, Oklahoma City, Bethany," and so on to California. These devices have the effect of generalizing the conflicts of the Joads, of making them representative of typical problems in a much wider social context. In every reversal, in every act of oppression, we feel the pressure of thousands.

If the film carries these striking equivalents of Steinbeck's prose, it is partly due to the assistance which Steinbeck offers the film-maker, partly to the visual imagination of the film-maker himself. Except for the freewheeling omniscience of the interchapters, the novel's prose relies wholly on dialogue and physical action to reveal character. Because Steinbeck's style is not marked by meditation, it resembles, in this respect, the classic form of the scenario. Even at moments of highest tension, Steinbeck scrupulously avoids getting inside the minds of his people. Here is Ma right after Tom has left her, and probably forever:

> "Good-by" she said, and she walked quickly away. Her footsteps were loud and careless on the leaves as she went through the brush. And as she went, out of the dim sky the rain began to fall, big drops and few, splashing on the dry leaves heavily. Ma stopped and stood still in the dripping thicket. She turned about—took three steps back toward the mound of vines; and then she turned quickly and went back toward the boxcar camp.

Although this is Steinbeck's characteristic style, it can also serve as precise directions for the actor. There is nothing here which cannot be turned into images of physical reality. Critics who seem surprised at the ease with which Steinbeck's work moves from one medium to another may find their explanation here. Precisely this fidelity to physical detail was responsible, for example, for the success [of] *Of Mice and Men* first as a novel, then as a play, then as a film. And yet, in *The Grapes of Wrath*, the film-makers rethought the material for themselves, and frequently found more exact cinematic keys to the mood and color of particular scenes in the book. Often their additions are most effective in areas where the novel is powerless—in moments of silence. Casy jumping over a fence and tripping, after the boast about his former preaching prowess; Ma Joad burning her keepsakes (the little dog from the St. Louis Exposition, the old letters, the card from Pa); the earrings which she saves, holding them to her ears in the cracked mirror, while the sound track carries the muted theme from "Red River Valley"; the handkerchiefs which Tom and Casy hold to their mouths in the gathering dust; Tom laboriously adding an "s" to "funerl" in the note which will accompany Grampa to his grave; the reflection of Al, Tom, and Pa in the jalopy's windshield at night as the family moved through the hot, eery desert—all these, while they have no precedent in the novel, make for extraordinarily effective cinema. The images are clean and precise, the filmic signature of a consistent collaboration between John Ford and his cameraman.

The deletions, on one level, are sacrifices to the exigencies of time and plot. The dialogue is severely pruned. Most of the anecdotes are dropped, along with the curse words. And the leisurely, discursive pace of the novel gives way to a tightly knit sequence of events. The episodes involving the traveling companionship of the Wilsons; the desertions of Noah and Connie; the repeated warnings about the dismal conditions in California from bitterly disappointed migrants who are traveling home the other way; and countless other small events do not appear in the film story, though a few of them, like Noah's desertion, appeared in the script and were even shot during production. But the moment we go from an enumeration of these deletions to the arrangement of sequences in the final work, we have come to our central structural problem.

As I indicated earlier, the structure of the book resembles a parabola in which the high point is the successful thwarting of the riot at the Government Camp. Beginning with Tom's desolate return to his abandoned house, the narrative proceeds through the journey from Oklahoma to California; the Hooverville episodes; the Government Camp episodes; the strike-breaking episodes at the Hooper Ranch; Tom's departure; the flooding of the cotton pickers' boxcar camp; the last scene in the abandoned farm. From the privation and dislocation of the earlier episodes, the Joads are continually plagued, threatened with dissolution, until, through the gradual knitting of strength and resistance, the family finds an identity which coincides with its experience at the Government Camp. Here they are startled by the sudden absence of everything from which they have been running—dirty living conditions, external compulsion, grubbing for survival, brutal policemen, unscrupulous merchants. They find, instead, a kind of miniature planned economy, efficiently run, boasting modern sanitation, self-government, co-operative living, and moderate prices. After their departure from the camp, the fortunes of the Joads progressively deteriorate, until that desolate ending which depicts Rose of Sharon's stillborn child floating downstream. The critical response to Steinbeck's shocking ending was almost universally negative. Clifton Fadiman called it the "tawdriest kind of fake symbolism."[18] Anthony West attributed it to the novel's

[18]Clifton Fadiman, "Highway 66—A Tale of Five Cities," *New Yorker*, XV (April 15, 1939), 81.

"astonishingly awkward" form.[19] Louis Kronenberger found that the entire second half of the book "lacks form and intensity . . . ceases to grow, to maintain direction,"[20] but did not locate the reasons for his dissatisfaction. Malcolm Cowley, in spite of general enthusiasm, found the second half less impressive than the first because Steinbeck "wants to argue as if he weren't quite sure of himself."[21] Charles Angoff was one of a small minority who defended both the ending and the "robust looseness" of the novel as squarely in the narrative tradition of Melville, Cervantes and Thomas Hardy.[22]

Contrast these objections with the general approval of the film's structure. Thomas Burton becomes adulatory over Ford's "incessant physical intimacy and fluency."[23] Otis Ferguson speaks in superlatives: "this is a best that has no very near comparison to date. . . . It all moves with the simplicity and perfection of a wheel across silk."[24] Why did the film-makers merit such a sharply contrasting critical reception? Simply because they corrected the objectionable structure of the novel. First, they deleted the final sequence; and second they accomplished one of the most remarkable narrative switches in film history. Instead of ending with the strike-breaking episodes in which Tom is clubbed, Casy killed, and the strikers routed, the film ends with the Government Camp interlude. This reversal, effected with almost surgical simplicity, accomplishes, in its metamorphic power, an entirely new structure which has far-reaching consequences. Combined with the deletion of the last dismal episode, and the pruning, alterations, and selections we have already traced, the new order changes the parabolic structure to a straight line that continually ascends. Beginning with the desolate scene of the dust storm, the weather in the film improves steadily with the fortunes of the Joads, until, at

---

[19]Anthony West, "The Grapes of Wrath," *New Statesman and Nations*, XVIII (September 16, 1939), 404–405.

[20]Louis Kronenberger, "Hungry Caravan: The Grapes of Wrath," *Nation,* CXLVIII (April 15, 1939), 441.

[21]Malcolm Cowley, "American Tragedy," *New Republic,* XCVIII (May 3, 1939), 382.

[22]Charles Angoff, "In the Great Tradition," *North American Review,* CCXLVII (Summer, 1939), 387.

[23]Thomas Burton, "Wine from These Grapes," *Saturday Review of Literature,* XXI (February 10, 1940), 16.

[24]Otis Ferguson, "Show for the People," *New Republic,* CII (February 12, 1940), 212.

the end, the jalopy leaves the Government Camp in sunlight with exuberant triumph. Even a sign, called for in the original script, which might have darkened the rosy optimism that surrounds the departing buggy, does not appear in the cut version. The sign was to have read, "No Help Wanted." As in the novel, Tom's departure is delayed until the end, but the new sequence of events endows his farewell speech with much more positive overtones. In place of the original ending, we find a line that appears at the end of Chapter XX, exactly two-thirds of the way through the book. It is Ma's strong assurance, "We'll go on forever, Pa. We're the people." On a thematic level, as Asheim points out, the affirmative ending implies that action is not required since the victims of the situation will automatically emerge triumphant. "Thus the book, which is an exhortation to action, becomes a film which offers reassurance that no action is required to insure the desired resolution of the issue."[25] But the film's conclusion has the advantage of seeming structurally more acceptable. Its "new logic" affords a continuous movement which, like a projectile, carries everything before it. The movie solution satisfies expectations which are there in the novel to begin with and which the novel's ending does not satisfactorily fulfill. Hence the critics' conflicting reaction to the two endings. Where the book seems to stop and meander in California, the film displays a forward propulsion that carries well on beyond the Colorado River.

Is such an inversion justified? Nunnally Johnson reports that he chose Ma's speech for his curtain line because he considered it the "real" spirit of Steinbeck's book.[26] This might seem at first like brazen tampering. But Johnson further reports that from Steinbeck himself he received *carte blanche* to make any alterations he wished. Steinbeck defended his position on the grounds that a novelist's final statement is in his book. Since the novelist can add nothing more, the film-maker is obliged to remake the work in his own style. If Steinbeck's awareness of the adaptational process is not enough, we may also find internal justification for the film-makers' brilliantly simple reversal. We have seen how the production crew effected alterations which mute the villainy of cops and tradesmen; underplay the religious satire; cloud over the novel's political radicalism. But part of this withdrawal has precedent in

[25]Asheim, p. 157.
[26]In an interview with the author.

the novel itself. The city man's portrayal of the anonymity of the banks; the proprietor's evasive answer to Tom in the Government Camp; Ma and Tom's mystical faith—these are all Steinbeck's. So is the fact that from the beginning Tom is on parole, which he technically breaks by leaving the state. Already he is outside the domain of legal ordinance. Tom is a fugitive who *has* to keep running. If the film's conclusion withdraws from a leftist commitment, it is because the novel does also. If the film vaporizes radical sociology, the novel withdraws from it, too, with Rose of Sharon's final act. The familial optimism of the one and the biological pessimism of the other are two sides of the same coin.

The structural achievement of the cinematic version may account, paradoxically, for the film's troubling reputation. On the one hand, acclamation, box-office success, critical enthusiasm; Jane Darwell winning an Academy Award for her portrayal of Ma Joad; the casting and acting of Henry Fonda, John Carradine, Charlie Grapewin, John Qualen, Frank Darien, Grant Mitchell, and the others, generally considered flawless; Nunnally Johnson sporting a gold plaque on the wall of his studio office in recognition of a fine screenplay; and one reporter poking fun at the grandiose premiere of the film at the Normandie Theater in New York, which was attended by glamorous stars adorned in jewels and furs, and, like a "Blue Book pilgrimage,"[27] by the representatives of the very banks and land companies that had tractored the Joads off their farms. Zanuck and his entourage must have known that the filmic portrait of Steinbeck's book was no serious threat.

On the other hand, the industry's discomfort. *The Grapes of Wrath* came as close as any film in Hollywood's prolific turnout to exposing the contradictions and inequities at the heart of American life. A new thing had been created and its implications were frightening. In spite of its facile conclusion, the film raises questions to which others, outside the fictive world, have had to supply answers. The film's unusual cinematographic accomplishments, its structural unity, its documentary realism, combine to fashion images, embodying those questions, which one may review with profit again and again. If the novel is remembered for its moral anger, the film is remembered for its beauty. And yet the industry

[27]Michael Mok, "Slumming with Zanuck," *Nation,* CL (February 3, 1940), 127–28.

has been a little embarrassed by its success. That success and that embarrassment may help explain why Nunnally Johnson has accomplished so little of lasting interest since his work on this film, and why he was last seen completing the scenario for Sloan Wilson's *The Man in the Gray Flannel Suit,* a book of a very different kind! It may explain why John Ford never lists *The Grapes of Wrath* as one of his favorite films, and why Ford himself offers perhaps the best explanation for the film's unique personality. Tersely, but with just the slightest trace of whimsy and bravado, John Ford remarks, "I never read the book."[28]

[28]In an interview with the author.

The Turtle or the Gopher:
Another Look at the Ending
of *The Grapes of Wrath*

by Stuart L. Burns

Critics generally agree that the parable of the turtle presented in chapter three of *The Grapes of Wrath* foreshadows and parallels the adventures of the Joad family. Almost as unanimously, they agree that the concluding scene of the novel dramatizes Steinbeck's theme that, as Ma Joad states it, "the people . . . go on."[1] To be sure, there has been considerable controversy about the propriety of the conclusion—whether it is dramatic, poignant, sentimental, vulgar, or obscene. But most scholars agree about its meaning. I am inclined to believe that the critics have correctly assessed Steinbeck's intent in both instances. But whatever his intent, this is not what he accomplished. For the affirmative parable of the turtle provides a contrast, not a parallel, to the tragic story of the Joads. And while the scene in which Rosasharn nurses the old man is certainly a logical ending to the novel, it is a much more pessimistic conclusion, thematically, than the phrase "the people go on" connotes. Had Steinbeck truly wanted a parable complementary to the story of the Joads and to the theme of the novel, he would have done better to have inserted the story of the gopher which appears, instead, in *Cannery Row*. For the point of that parable is that peace and prosperity are attainable only if one is willing to sacrifice love and companionship. The price one pays for community is the threat of famine, flood and violent death.

"The Turtle or the Gopher: Another Look at the Ending of *The Grapes of Wrath*" by Stuart L. Burns. From *Western American Literature,* 9 (1974): 53–57. Reprinted by permission of the editors.
[1]*The Grapes of Wrath* (New York: The Viking Press, 1958), p. 383. All subsequent quotations from the novel will refer to this edition, and page numbers will be included in the text.

That is a drastically simplified, but not inaccurate summary of a major theme in *The Grapes of Wrath*.

There are certain similarities between the turtle and the Joads, of course: it is heading southwest, as will they; the highway (but not the same highway) is a formidable obstacle to both; and the overloaded Hudson certainly travels at a turtle's pace. But consider the very real and thematically more meaningful distinctions. The turtle has an instinctive sense of purpose and direction; it turns "aside for nothing" (20). And while one cannot know for certain where the turtle is going or what it intends to do when it gets there, the context clearly implies that it *will* get there and accomplish whatever it has instinctively set out to do. The Joads, on the other hand, head southwest due to circumstances beyond their control. They have at first no desire to move at all, and throughout a nostalgia for the Oklahoma farm they were forced to leave. And only an unflagging optimist would connect their concluding situation, or for that matter their future prospects, with any concrete achievement. But perhaps the most significant distinction between the turtle and the Joads is that, whereas the former plays a fertilizing role to the "sleeping life waiting to be dispersed" (20), the life that Rosasharn carries is delivered premature and stillborn. Twelve Joads spanning three generations (thirteen spanning four if one counts the unborn baby) begin the journey; although ten presumably survive, only six are together at the end. The emphasis is on attrition, not continuance.

If one examines subsequent passages in the novel where the turtle is alluded to, the difference between the positive thrust of the parable and the negative thrust of the narrative becomes even clearer. Two characters, Tom Joad and Jim Casy, are specifically associated with the turtle. Tom picks it up and carries it with him for a while (to the northeast, opposite the turtle's intended direction); and Casy's physical description is suggestive of a turtle. He has a "long head, bony, tight of skin, and set on a neck as stringy and muscular as a celery stalk." His "heavy . . . protruding" eyeballs with lids stretched to cover them" (25) are decidedly reptilian. That Tom and Casy should be closely associated with the turtle is appropriate inasmuch as, of the thirteen people who trek west in the Hudson, these two do develop a sense of purpose and direction akin to the turtle's. But the analogy has its limits. The turtle survives its encounter with the hostile forces of civilization. Indeed, the truck which swerves to hit it actually flips it across the highway, aiding it in this hazardous crossing. Casy, who has no protective shell into which he can withdraw his head, has it crushed by a pick handle wielded by the leader of the mob at the Hooper ranch. And while Tom survives on this occasion, his future—a hunted ex-convict turned labor agitator—bodes nothing but ill. The text suggests that the turtle will survive because it expends its energies totally in its self-interest; Casy dies because he devotes his energies to helping others.

This distinction between self-interest and humanitarianism is further illustrated in another brief scene in which Granma is associated with the turtle. The red ant which crawls "over the folds of loose skin on her neck" (286) while she is dying recalls the ant the turtle crushes inside its shell (20). But, whereas the turtle reacts savagely and effectively, Granma is able to do no more than feebly scratch her face. To be sure, Ma Joad crushes the ant "between thumb and forefinger" (286), in a gesture reminiscent of the turtle's action. But this only reinforces the point that, as Tom Joad states later, "a fella ain't no good alone" (570).

The point of difference can be illustrated in terms of one other dominant motif in the novel. Animals are indifferent to and can survive the damage done by machines. The Joads' house cat turns wild and remains on the tenant farm. The turtle is actually aided by the truck whose driver tries to kill it. The Joads, by contrast, are first displaced by machines, then rendered helplessly dependent on the Hudson to get them to California. And while an occasional person like Muley Graves may exist as does the house cat,[2] there is no character whose pattern of behavior is suggestive of the indomitable will of the turtle. If there is one character in the novel who seems most likely to survive and make a decent life for himself, that would have to be Al Joad. But Al will succeed only if he has the callousness to wrest himself free of family dependence on him—he is the only remaining member who can drive the truck—and get himself that dreamed-of job in a garage. That is to say, he can survive by joining the side that owns and runs the machines; by acting, in short, a little less like a decent human being and a little more like the turtle.

Yet there is no denying that a central theme in the novel is, as a number of reputable critics have noted, "the education of the Joad

---

[2]But, even here, his name has a connotation negative to the idea of survival.

family ... towards an ideal of cooperation."[3] But this theme is essentially contradictory to the turtle parable which is most certainly a statement in praise of rugged individualism. Is it possible, then, that Steinbeck intended the turtle interchapter to be thematic counterpoint rather than parallel? The evidence suggests the contrary. As Edmund Wilson noted, the Joads exist "almost on the animal level." Their progress to California "is accompanied and parodied ... by animals, insects and birds."[4] And Steinbeck obviously views with benevolence their instinctive attitudes toward sex, death, and the natural functions of the body. Thus, we are led to the conclusion that the contradiction illustrates, not Steinbeck's control of his material, but a fundamental and irreconcilable ambivalence in his philosophy: his sympathy for communism combined but not compatible with his nostalgic admiration for Jeffersonian agrarian individualism;[5] his trust in "the people" and his equal distrust of any kind of organization.

And this brings us finally to the question of the effectiveness of the concluding scene in the barn—a scene which presents a dramatic tableau of the trap the Joads are in. Theodore Pollock has argued that the episode successfully completes the novel's thematic movement from a beginning point of sterility to a concluding point of fertility or reproduction.[6] I would suggest the case is precisely the opposite. The rain produces not an end to the drought, but a life-destroying flood. This is not gentle spring rain, but a winter downpour. And while, afterward, nature may be "pale green with the beginning year" (592), the Joads will have "no kinda work for three months" (591). Furthermore, while Rosasharn's nursing the old man may cause us to marvel at the human capacity for love under the most adverse circumstances, there is nothing to suggest continuance of life on the human level. I can perhaps best make my point by way of analogy. William Faulkner's *Light in*

[3]Jules Chametzky, "The Ambivalent Endings of *The Grapes of Wrath*," *Modern Fiction Studies,* 11 (Spring, 1965), 36. See also Warren French, *John Steinbeck* (New York: Twayne, 1961), pp. 100–01, and Peter Lisca, "*The Grapes of Wrath* as Fiction," *PLMA,* 72 (March, 1957), 305.

[4]*Classics and Commercials* (New York: Farrar, Straus & Co., 1950), pp. 35–36.

[5]Cf. Chester Eisenger, "Jeffersonian Agrarianism in *The Grapes of Wrath*," *The University of Kansas City Review,* 14 (Winter, 1947), 149–54.

[6]"On the Ending of *The Grapes of Wrath*," *Modern Fiction Studies*, 4 (Summer, 1958), 177–78.

August concludes on an affirmative note because the symbolic connection stemming from Mrs. Hines's confusion of Lena Grove's
newborn baby with Joe Christmas suggests that a new generation
may rise above the errors and frailties of the old. In *The Grapes of
Wrath*, the inverted-Madonna symbol suggests no such affirmation. There is a salvaging of a life, but no re-birth. All of the first
and fourth generations of Joads are dead, a detail which implies
that the rest are trapped in their present circumstances. The Moses
who might have fulfilled some future promise floats stillborn in
the willows.

The conclusion to *The Grapes of Wrath* functions much as does
the conclusion to Mark Twain's *Huckleberry Finn*. As readers, we
may respond positively to the last few sentences. But if we consider the conclusion in relation to the total context of the novel, we
see it as a thin veneer of affirmation concealing a logical and
inexorable movement toward tragedy or pathos. Intended as positive upbeat, the episode only illustrates the more forcibly Steinbeck's inability to see where his novel came out, thematically. But in
his unawareness or ambivalence, Steinbeck demonstrates himself
a writer highly reflective of the American culture. Like him,
American society has never been able to integrate or resolve its
contradictory impulse to admire the self-reliant man, while at the
same time it pressures him to conform or, at the least, to be con-
siderate of the needs and wishes of his fellow men. Individualism
is not compatible with cooperation. As countless works of literature from the time of Sophocles' *Antigone* to Ralph Ellison's *In-
visible Man* have demonstrated, the individual must always suffer
some measure of conflict with social order. Therefore, if each man
is, as Casy speculates, a small part of "one big soul" (33), then his
path through life can never be as simple *or* as successful as the
turtle's. Like the gopher he must pay a price for love. In the fact
that "a fella ain't no good alone" lies both his tragedy and his
humanity.

A New Consideration
of the Intercalary Chapters
in *The Grapes of Wrath*

by Mary Ellen Caldwell

Critical opinions have differed, often sharply, about the function and effectiveness of the intercalary chapters in *The Grapes of Wrath* by John Steinbeck.[1] These are the chapters which do not directly advance the narrative of the Joad family, but which, intercalated between the chapters of the narrative power, give that narrative increased depth and broader significance. The opening chapter likewise, though because of its position it can scarcely be called intercalary, performs the same function.

Until recently, it was fairly generally agreed that the novel lacked continuity. However, opinion is now moving toward a willingness to view it as a carefully worked out structural whole.[2] At the risk of going against Steinbeck's specific injunction,[3] I wish to point out

"A New Consideration of the Intercalary Chapters in *The Grapes of Wrath*" by Mary Ellen Caldwell. From the *Markham Review*, 3 (1973) 115–19. Reprinted by permission of the editor and author.

[1]These opinions are adequately summarized in E. W. Tedlock, Jr., and C. V. Wicker, *Steinbeck and His Critics, A Record of Twenty-Five Years* (University of New Mexico Press: Albuquerque, 1957).

[2]Evidence that Steinbeck made use of unifying devices is shown in *The Pastures of Heaven* where he has a store keeper suggest that maybe the curse of the place, Battle farm, and Bert Munroe's personal curse of ill luck have gone underground, like a pair of rattlesnakes in a gopher hole, and that later a lot of baby curses will come crawling around the valley. Then the succeeding chapters show these baby curses emerging in separate stories, but tying the book together as a whole.

[3]*The Colorado Quarterly* published two essays on Steinbeck: Bernard Bowron, "The Grapes of Wrath: a 'Wagons West' Romance," III (1954), 84–91, and Warren G. French, "Another look at 'The Grapes of Wrath,' " III, (1955), 337–343. Mr. Steinbeck, responding to an invitation to comment on these essays, wrote "A Letter on Criticism," IV (1955), 218–219, in which he said: "I don't think the *Grapes of Wrath* is obscure in what it tries to say. As to its classification

the close unity of the book, to show how one chapter prepares for and flows into the next, and to consider in detail one segment of the skeletal structure, Chapter 15, which epitomizes the whole novel.

This chapter caught the attention of Claude-Edmonde Magny, who without expanding on its full significance felt that it had a slight connection with the plot proper but for poetic reasons was significant to the complete work.[4] Peter Lisca, who maintains that the novel does have structural form and who treats the intercalary chapters at some length to show this, makes no particular mention of Chapter 15.[5] I see this chapter as being more than just one of the sixteen intercalary chapters which "amplify the pattern of action created by the Joad family," or providing historical information (Lisca, p. 156).

There are thirty chapters in the novel. They follow a regular pattern of alternation between impersonal, panoramic accounts of conditions or social forces and the Joad story proper. To show the effectiveness of the carefully planned structure, and to point up Steinbeck's conscious handling of sequences, it is necessary to note in some detail what he does with these alternating chapters.[6]

Chapter 1 sets a mood of impending disaster. In Oklahoma, women watch their men to see if they will break under the strain of the drought which is slowly but steadily ravaging the state. Chapter 2 introduces Tom Joad, who has just been paroled from the state penitentiary and is going home after an absence of four years, unaware of what has been happening to his parents and the other children. In intercalary Chapter 3 the persistence of the life force is seen in the way that every seed is supplied with the "anlage of movement." The land turtle, crawling southwest, clamps down on a wild oat head, carries it a distance, drops it, covers it with dirt as he crawls on. In Chapter 4 Tom encounters Jim Casy, a former

---

and pickling, I have neither opinion nor interest. It's just a book, interesting I hope, instructive in the same way the writing instructed me. *Its structure is very carefully worked out* (italics mine) and it is no more intended to be inspected than the skeletal structure of a pretty girl. Just read it, don't count it!"

[4] In an essay translated by Francoise Gourier as "Steinbeck, or the Limits of the Impersonal Novel" from *L'Age du Roman Americain* (Paris, 1948), in Tedlock and Wicker, pp. 220–221.

[5] Peter Lisca, *The Wide World of John Steinbeck* (New Brunswick, N.J., 1958), pp. 156–160.

[6] All page references to the novel itself are to the Viking Press edition, Copyright 1939, Nineteenth Printing, July, 1964.

preacher whom he has known before. In their conversation, Tom indicates that the life force is strong in him, as it is in Casy. "Maybe it ain't a sin. Maybe it's just the way folks is" (p. 31). Discarding his orthodox religion, Casy has arrived at a concept of the oversoul (as Emerson did, by intuition). To further illustrate the strength of the life force, Tom recalls how his Uncle John when he wanted pig, wanted a whole pig, and ate until he was gorged. As Tom and Casy approach the Joad place, they see that the house is at an angle, askew on its foundation. Chapter 5 (intercalary) gives a picture of how banks and large land companies are "tractoring off" the tenant farmers who were once owners of the land. The great tractors, moving like insects, are a mechanized version of the life force, an adaptation to changing economic conditions. The tractor driver is given a bonus if he by seeming accident knocks a house over to encourage a family to move. Some local young men see a chance to survive by becoming tractor drivers. It is a means to feed their families.

The Joad story continues in Chapter 6 with Jim Casy and Tom learning from Muley Graves, who drifts by like a graveyard ghost, that the family has gone to Uncle John's to prepare for going to California, for joining the trek of hundreds of thousands of dispossessed people crossing the country in jalopies. The bitter, staccato intercalary Chapter 7 presents a picture of used car dealers, who know that the bonanza will not last for them. They are determined to "soak it to them," to sell the rolling junk for as high a price as possible. Following Chapter 7, Pa's making over the cutdown sedan into a truck takes on much more significance as the Joad story is resumed in Chapter 8. But even with a truck, such a large family will not be able to carry many of its belongings.

The junk dealers in Chapter 9 are not buying junk, they are buying "junked lives," bitterness, years of hard work, "a sorrow that can't talk." An imaginary speaker asks, "How can we live without our lives? How will we know it's us without our past?" (p. 120). The disastrous sacrifice in Chapter 10 of the Joad property—horses, wagons, tools, household goods—becomes more credible after Chapter 9. Tom says to his mother that he knew a fellow from California in jail who said that there were already too many people out there. But they go on. The truck becomes the new "hearth," the active thing, the "living principle" (p. 135), carefully tended by Al, the younger son who hears the brakes squeal, watches the oil gauge, and knows the thinness of the tires. Chapter 11, intercalary, supplies a fitting end to the Oklahoma section. A vacant house quickly deteriorates; mice move in and stow their seeds in corners, back of drawers; seeds spring up in front of the door step, and grass grows through the cracks in the floor. The life force persists in a different form.

The pattern of regularly alternating intercalary and narrative chapters is here broken, for Chapter 12 is also intercalary, opening the second major phase of the novel, the journey to California as Chapter 1 did the Oklahoma section. Highway 66 is the pathway of flight. Jalopies converge upon it from all tributaries. People in fine cars from the East, going west because of curiosity or boredom; dispossessed families, desperate but hopeful—all are going along Highway 66. Here is a general foreshadowing of what they are to find in California: "Fella says you're just as free as you got jack to pay for it. . . . You go steal that tire an' you're a thief, but he tried to steal your four dollars for a busted tire. They call that sound business" (pp. 163–164). Some have cruel experiences; some have beautiful ones, renewing their faith in the essential goodness of man.

The Joads' experiences on the road continue in Chapter 13. Their dog is killed on the highway; they make friends with the Wilsons from Kansas; and Grampa dies and is quietly buried in a field. In intercalary Chapter 14, the nervousness of the Western states under the beginning change is depicted.

Then comes the second interruption in the pattern of regularly alternating chapters. Chapter 15, descriptive, expository, and containing its own independent but fully sketched narrative, is unique and central to the story, an epitome of the whole work. But before considering this chapter in detail, it is better to complete the presentation of the overall pattern.

In Chapter 16 the Joads and the Wilsons travel together. The shadow of a buzzard slides across the earth as they pull over to the side of the road to repair the Wilsons' car. Casy, still traveling with them, senses the nervousness, the unfriendly restlessness of the western country. Tom and Al come face to face with it at a used parts junk yard. Tom meets it again in his encounter with the inhospitable man who runs the camp ground where they have to pay fifty cents a night. In the same camp ground, the Joads also meet a returning, disillusioned emigrant, who bitterly realizes that they will not listen to him but must find out for themselves.

In intercalary Chapter 17, people in migrant camps for the

night are forced to evolve a new way of life that necessitates a new code of behavior. In the morning the jalopies scuttle out onto the highway like bugs, but toward night they again cluster like bugs near shelter and water.[7] Each night a new community is formed of agrarian folk who have now become migrant folk, evolving new social patterns.

The narrative is continued in Chapter 18. The Joads cross Arizona, stopping beside the road at night. They cross the Colorado River at Topock and are actually in California, but they will not feel that they are really there until they cross the desert and look down on the lush, green valley of fruit and promise. At Needles, Mrs. Wilson is too ill to continue, so the families separate. Noah Joad, the oldest son, "strange" since birth from a possible brain damage, tells Tom that he is not going on, that he is going to stay with the river, and he walks away. Granma dies upon the load with only Ma knowing it as the family crosses the desert at night. When they are stopped at Daggett for agricultural inspection, Ma objects to unloading, because she says Granma is ill. The officer takes one look and sends them on to Barstow. But they do not stop there; they go on until they can see the valley. Then Ma tells the rest of the family.

Structurally, this is the end of the second part, the journey. The third, the California part, is opened by intercalary Chapter 19, telling how land-hungry American squatters moved in and took the land away from the Mexicans. The squatters' children gradually lost hunger for the land, and absentee landowners took it over as big business. Then the migrants moved in like scurrying ants, 250,000 to 300,000 of them. On the edge of every town is a Hooverville; in every town the deputies are determined that the squatters shall keep moving, that they shall not be allowed to put down roots or to organize. Chapter 20 picks up the Joads in their first Hooverville and tells of their first encounter with the deputies. After a confrontation, Casy is arrested and taken to jail, and Tom must hide out. Rose of Sharon, the Joad daughter, and her husband have sharp words about conditions, and he walks off, though she is pregnant. In intercalary Chapter 21, the migrant people change when their children are hungry and they are met

[7]The recurring insect motif is noted by Robert J. Griffin and Wm. E. Freeman, "Machines and Animals: Pervasive Motifs in *The Grapes of Wrath*," *Journal of English and Germanic Philology*, LXII, 569–580.

with hostility. The great landowners, who also own canneries, want a plentiful labor supply and low wages. There is a thin line between hunger and anger. The Joads, in Chapter 22, learn how a government migrant camp is run, how it is resented by the large landowners, and how the small landowners are forced out of business. After intercalary Chapter 23, showing the migrants humbly seeking their simple pleasures in story-telling, music, and dancing, the Joads (Chapter 24) help foil an attempt to break up a dance.

Many men have labored to produce better varieties of plants. A fruitful year comes, and the harvest is plentiful (Chapter 25). But "Men who have created new fruits in the world cannot create a system whereby their fruits may be eaten" (p. 476). "And children dying of pellagra must die because a profit cannot be taken from an orange. . . . In the souls of the people the grapes of wrath are filling and growing heavy, growing heavy for the vintage" (p. 477).

The Joads have to leave the migrant camp to seek work farther north (Chapter 26). At the Wheeler ranch, Tom Joad sees Casy, who has been released from jail and is now organizing the migrants, killed by a deputy. Tom kills the killer and goes into hiding, while the family moves on a short distance to pick cotton. Cotton pickers (intercalary Chapter 27) are wanted, for the more pickers, the lower the wage for picking. A picker must buy his own bag, and each job requires a new bag. One fellow never did get a bag paid for. In Chapter 28 Ruthie Joad, aged twelve, brags about her brother, who has killed two men and is now hiding out. Ma feels that Tom must go farther away than the nearby cave in which he has taken refuge. In the dark, womb-like cave, Tom tells his mother that he will be wherever there is a fight for justice (p. 572). Ma goes home to learn that Al wants to marry Aggie Wainwright, the daughter of another migrant. The life force goes on, even under adverse conditions. Rose of Sharon, pregnant and discouraged, determines to pick cotton (to force a miscarriage?). Not all seeds grow to maturity; some fall on barren ground or are uprooted.

When rains come (intercalary Chapter 29), the migrant families are marooned in tents or in boxcars. Some carrying children and old people go looking for abandoned barns or houses. Frustrated by hunger, sickness, and unemployment, men beg first, then steal. Comfortable people in houses feel pity at first, but that changes to distaste, and then finally to hatred for the migrants. If a man had a team of horses working for him, he would not turn them out to starve until he needed them again but he feels no responsibility for migrant workers. The women watch their men to see if they will break. When fear goes out of their faces and anger comes, the women are reassured (echo of Chapter 1). When the rains stop, the growth cycles begin anew with returning green.

The novel ends with a narrative chapter. Uncle John puts Rose of Sharon's baby, born dead, in an apple box to float down the stream and rot in the street to show the landowners how conditions are. The family, having climbed out to higher ground, reach a barn where Rose of Sharon with full breasts gives suck to an old man dying of hunger. Even here the life force continues to manifest itself (echoes of earlier chapters).

Because the intercalary chapters have unified and strengthened the whole in theme by the imagery and recurrent motifs deployed in them, the final chapter that many critics have felt was unsatisfactory completes the whole by rounding the circle. As Ma Joad earlier tells Tom "us people will go on livin' when all them people is gone. Why, Tom, we're the people that live" (p. 383).

Chapter 15 is placed in the center of the book, by chapter count, not by page count. It is neither a purely intercalary chapter as the others are nor is it a part of the Joad narrative. It is an epitome of the whole book, having its own narrative paragraphs and intercalary paragraphs.

Steinbeck starts out with a panoramic view of hamburger stands, or cafe-gas stations, in general, along Highway 66. They all look alike. Minnie or Susy or Mae are "middle-aging behind the counter" while Joe or Carl or Al, wearing the white cook's hat, slap down hamburgers. In the same paragraph Steinbeck moves smoothly from the general to the specific. "He [Al] repeats Mae's orders gently, scrapes the griddle, wipes it down with burlap. Moody and silent" (p. 209).

From now on to the end, the chapter is a narrative of its own, involving Mae and Al and the people who stop at their stand. There are frequent intercalary paragraphs that serve to unify the chapter and also to relate it to the whole book.

Mae, who is the contact with the public, shows a definite preference for truck drivers, who constitute the backbone of the regular trade. When they come she exchanges banter and rough jokes with them. Al never speaks; he is content; he cooks. In the meantime traffic is constant: "Cars whisking by on 66. License plates. Mass., Tenn., R. I., N.Y., Vt., Ohio. Going west. Fine cars, cruising at sixty-five" (p. 210).

Nine brief intercalary paragraphs follow depicting an imaginary conversation between any group of customers at any of the hamburger stands, remarking on the different kinds of cars from Cords to jalopies, their speed and merits.

A fuller intercalary paragraph describes the "Languid, heat-raddled ladies" (p. 210) who ride in big cars, laden down with accoutrements to improve their looks, move their bowels, insure their sex life being unproductive—all apart from their clothes. Artificiality and sterility have long since stifled any regenerative life force here. The description continues in two additional intercalary paragraphs: one, still on women in big cars who are bra-ed, girdled, sullen, discontented, selfish, and bored; the other, on men who accompany such women, men who are pot-bellied, puzzled, worried, insecure, but who are reassured in lodges and clubs that business is "not the curious ritualized thievery they know it is" (p. 211).

Then Steinbeck focuses on one woman and one man, going to California, just for the sake of being able to return home and say they had been there, casually dropping Hollywood gossip for effect. They cruise along at sixty in a big car. The woman, wanting a drink, wonders if it would be clean in this godforsaken country. She is typical of the Ugly American who travels and complains of facilities. When they stop at Al and Mae's, a personalized couple of the stereotyped rich come together with a personalized couple of the hamburger stand owners. The customers order very little, but complain and make themselves generally obnoxious, and then go on. Mae had seen this type of customer, when she worked in a hotel in Albuquerque, carry off towels, soap dishes, anything. She prefers truck drivers and hopes that the approaching transport will stop.

Then follows a conversation between a truck driver, Big Bill, and his helper, who plan to stop at Al and Mae's, and do. Big Bill exchanges risque banter with Mae, telling off-color jokes while the helper puts a nickel in the phonograph, plays the slot machine and walks to the counter.

To Steinbeck, not all mechanization is bad. He mentions the sound of machines working to good advantage: the phonograph, the coffee urn, the ice machine, and the electric fan. In fact, earlier in Chapter 14, Steinbeck had an imaginary character ask, "Is a tractor bad? Is the power that turns the long furrow wrong? If this tractor were ours it would be good" (p. 205).

Mae mentions that a Massachusetts car had stopped earlier. Big Bill says there are many cars, all going west. The helper describes a wreck they had seen that morning in which a fellow in a Cadillac, doing ninety, ploughed into a cut-down car full of family and household goods, killing one child, and filling the air with bed-clothes, kids and chickens. In their general conversation they wonder where they all come from, where they all go; Mae repeats the rumor that the poor people steal, but she says that she and Al have lost nothing so far. Here is foreshadowing of the fear the local people come to have of the migrants as shown in the later chapters.

Just then a 1926 Nash pulls off to stop. The back seat is piled nearly to the ceiling with household stuff. Two boys are sitting on the load. With a mattress and a folded tent on top of the car, tent poles along the running board, a whole family and their pos-sessions are in transit—like the Joads. A man gets out of the car, comes to the door and politely and humbly asks if he can get some water. The boys have already scrambled out and gone to the hose, and are digging their toes in the mud puddle. In Chapter 4 (p. 23), Tom Joad took his shoes off and worked his damp feet into the hot dry dust. In Chapter 30 (p. 616), Ma and Rose of Sharon "plowed through the mud." In many instances, throughout the book, the poor people stay in close touch with the soil.

After getting the water, the man wants to buy a loaf of bread for ten cents. Mae demurs—they would run short themselves and besides a loaf of bread costs fifteen cents. Threatened by growls, then snarls from Al if she doesn't, Mae sells them a loaf for ten cents, as well as two five cent sticks of candy for a penny. The man has his pride. He does not want charity, but he has far to go. (The Joads had to hoard their money. They had to turn Granma's body over to the authorities for a county burial, although Pa did pay five dollars to have a painted board put up [p. 341].) The Nash leaves the hamburger stand in a blue cloud, obviously burning oil. It is symbolic of all the jalopies in poor condition being nursed to get to California. (In the Joad family, Al assumes an importance a teen-ager might not otherwise have, for he knows about cars.)

The truck drivers have overheard the conversation in Al and Mae's place and when they go on their way they leave a generous tip. Mae contrasts them with the Massachusetts couple. (Ma Joad once mentioned that you will get help from your own people [pp. 513–514]. It was a truck driver in Chapter 2 who gave Tom a ride.)

Al, the cook, has been generous, but he is also shrewdly calculating. He knows that it is time for the slot machine three to pay off so he plays it until it does, then puts the money in the till. Mae wonders what they'll do in California. Al asks, "Who?" Traffic continues to whiz by. Another transport stops and Mae goes into her routine of welcome.

Chapter 15 is not only a microcosm of *The Grapes of Wrath* but also a microcosm of the United States. Al and Mae's stand could have been on any highway. The rich, traveling in highpowered cars, crashed into poor families. The dispossessed and land hungry ones sought new homes but they still had their pride. They wanted work, not charity. Both generosity and selfish conniving came from unexpected sources. The artificiality and sterility of those removed from direct contact with the common segment of society is contrasted sharply with the persistence of the life force in the poor who ask for bread. The young boys looked at the candy not with any real hope but with great longing. The machine age uprooted man but it also brought changes that were beneficial. The big transports symbolized the far-reaching extent of commerce and trade, and they continued to come.

In looking back now on the structure of the book one can see the consistently worked out plan of alternating social and economic observations with chapters of a narrative, each augmenting the effect of the other, with a crystalization of the whole, placed in the center, confirming Steinbeck's own word that the structure was very carefully worked out.

Machines and Animals:
Pervasive Motifs
in *The Grapes of Wrath*

by Robert J. Griffin
and William A. Freedman

Once the hubbub over John Steinbeck's "propaganda tract" began to die down—there are still those who refuse to let it die completely—critics began to pay serious attention to *The Grapes of Wrath* as a work of art.[1] Such aspects of the novel as its characterization (whether or not the Joads are "cardboard figures"), the prose style (actually the several prose styles, but particularly the poetic effectiveness of the descriptive passages), and the interrelationship of the different kinds of chapters[2] have been discussed at some length. In this paper we should like to concentrate on two pervasive motifs in the novel, namely, the crucially important motifs of *machines* and *animals* which contribute considerably to structure and thematic content. We may call these two the "dominant motifs," but we must remember that extracting

"Machines and Animals: Pervasive Motifs in *The Grapes of Wrath*" by Robert J. Griffin and William A. Freedman. From *Journal of English and Germanic Philology*, 62 (July 1963), 569–80. Copyright 1963 by the Board of Trustees of the University of Illinois. Reprinted by permission of the publisher and the authors.

[1]For discussion of the criticism about Steinbeck's work, see Peter Lisca, *The Wide World of John Steinbeck* (New Brunswick, N.J., 1958), and E. W. Tedlock, Jr., and C. V. Wicker, *Steinbeck and His Critics* (Albuquerque, 1956). Lisca's treatment of the criticism serves as his introductory chapter and centers on the lamentable preoccupation with Steinbeck's social and philosophical attitudes and the consequent neglect of his artistry. Tedlock and Wicker's is likewise introductory and similarly oriented, closing with the hopeful conviction that "future critics will find him to be an artist with an artist's intentions, methods, and stature" (p. xli). The most recent and comprehensively excellent study of the novels is Warren French, *John Steinbeck* (New York, 1961).

[2]See Lisca (pp. 159 ff.) for discussion of Steinbeck's success at integrating different kinds of chapters into a unified though complex structure.

these elements is necessarily an act of oversimplification; it is only through their complex relationships with subsidiary motifs and devices, and with the more straightforward narration and exposition and argumentation, that they provide major symbols integral to the art and substance of the novel.[3] With this qualification in mind, we may proceed to a consideration of machines and animals as sources of tropes, as signs and underscoring devices, and ultimately as persistent symbols.

Very few of the tropes of the novel—the metaphors, similes, and allusions—make use of machinery as such. "Tractored out" is of course a prominent figure of speech repeated several times to express the Okies' plight in being forced from their plots of land by the mechanical monstrosity of industrialized farming ("tractored off" also appears a couple of times). But otherwise about the only instance of a metaphorical use of machinery is a single simile late in the novel: the weary men trying to build a bank of earth to hold back the flood "worked jerkily, like machines."[4] There are a good many metaphors applied to mechanical apparatuses—that is, tropes in which machinery is characterized by some non-mechanical phenomenon as the vehicle of the metaphor. Generally this metaphorical characterization of machines emphasizes animalism, or the bestial side of human affairs, as the seeders are said to rape the land. Fundamentally these metaphors appear designed to contribute to a general sense of tragedy or disaster indicated by such secondary motifs as the blood tropes—"the sun was as red as ripe new blood" (p. 6), "the earth was bloody in [the sun's] setting light" (p. 129)—and the frequent recurrence of "cut"—"the sun cut into the shade" (p. 10), "the road was cut with furrows" (p. 23).

While there are very few machine tropes, animal tropes abound. Often animals are used to characterize the human sex drive: Muley Graves (whose name is not inappropriate here) refers to himself during his first experiences as "snortin' like a buck deer, randy as a billygoat" (p. 69); young, virile Al Joad has been "a-billy-

---

[3]A really thorough exegesis of the novel would have to describe the many secondary devices interwoven with the major motifs: the significance of clothing, e.g., particularly hats—the gradual metamorphosis of the cheap new cap Tom gets on leaving prison, Uncle John's defacement of his old hat as he prepares to lose himself in drink, etc. The Biblical allusions—though not a "motif" in our sense—are of course an essential part of the novel.

[4]John Steinbeck, *The Grapes of Wrath* (New York: The Modern Library, 1939), p. 600. Subsequent page references are given in parentheses within the text.

goatin' aroun' the country. Tom-cattin' hisself to death" (p. 111).
And the sexuality of animals several times appears as the vehicle of
a metaphor: Casy refers to a participant in a revival meeting
as "jumpy as a stud horse in a box stall" (p. 38). Animal tropes
frequently serve to denote violence or depravity in human behavior: fighting "like a couple of cats" (p. 27); a tractor hitting a
share-cropper's cabin "give her a shake like a dog shakes a rat"
(p. 62); Muley used to be "mean like a wolf" but now is "mean like
a weasel" (p. 78); and Ma Joad describes Purty Boy Floyd's career
as comparable to a maddened animal at bay—"they shot at him
like a varmint, an' he shot back, an' then they run him like a
coyote, an' him a-snappin' an' a-snarlin,' mean as a lobo" (p. 103).
Animal tropes may simply indicate a harmless playfulness or
swagger: Winfield Joad is "kid-wild and calfish" (p. 129), and Al
acts like "a dung-hill rooster" (p. 575). But the most frequent and
significant use of the numerous animal tropes is to characterize
the Okies' plight: the Joads are forced off their forty acres, forced
to live "piled in John's house like gophers in a winter burrow"
(p. 63); then they begin an abortive trip toward what they hope will
prove to be a "New Canaan" in California, and Casy uses this tacit
analogy to describe the impersonal, industrial economy from
which they are fleeing:

> "Ever see one a them Gila monsters take hold, mister? Grabs hold,
> an' you chop him in two an' his head hangs on. Chop him at the
> neck an' his head hangs on. Got to take a screw-driver an' pry his
> head apart to git him loose. An' while he's layin' there, poison is
> drippin' an' drippin' into the hole he's made with his teeth." (p.
> 175)

Casy argues that the wrong results from men not staying "harnessed" together in a common effort ("mankin' was holy when it
was one thing"); one man can get "the bit in his teeth an' run off
his own way, kickin' an' draggin' an' fightin' " (p. 110). Consequently the roads to California are "full of frantic people running
like ants" (p. 324—the "ants" simile appears again, for instance,
on p. 388). In California the Okies work, when they can get
work, "like draft horses" (p. 601); they are driven "like pigs"
(p. 522) and forced to live "like pigs" (p. 571). Casy has been
observing and listening to the Okies in their misfortunes, and he
knows their fear and dissatisfaction and restlessness: "I hear 'em
an' feel 'em; an' they're beating their wings like a bird in a attic.

Gonna bust their wings on a dusty winda tryin' ta get out" (p. 34).

It should be noted that the animalistic references to people are not as a rule unfavorable ("randy as a billygoat" is scarcely a pejorative in Steinbeck's lusty lexicon). The few derogatory animal tropes are almost all applied to the exploiters (banks, land companies, profiteers) and not to the exploited (the Joads and other Okies). That these latter must behave like the lower animals is not their fault. Their animalism is the result of the encroachments of the machine economy. Machines, then, are frequently depicted as evil objects: they "tear in and shove the croppers out" (p. 13); "one man on a tractor can take the place of twelve or fourteen families" (p. 44); so the Okies must take to the road, seeking a new home, lamenting, "I lost my land, a single tractor took my land" (p. 206). Farming has become a mechanized industry, and Steinbeck devotes an entire chapter (nineteen) to the tragic results:

> The tractors which throw men out of work, the belt lines which carry loads, the machines which produce, all were increased; and more and more families scampered on the highways, looking for crumbs from the great holdings, lusting after the land beside the roads. The great owners formed associations for protection and they met to discuss ways to intimidate, to kill, to gas. (p. 325)

The Okies are very aware of the evils brought about by mechanization. Reduced to picking cotton for bare-subsistence wages, they realize that even this source of income may soon go. One asks, "Heard 'bout the new cotton-pickin' machine?" (p. 556).

The Joads find themselves living—trying to live—in an age of machinery. Machines or mechanized devices quite naturally play important roles in the symbolism of the novel. ("Symbolism" is here understood to mean the employment of concrete images—objects and events—to embody or suggest abstract qualities or concepts.) Some machines serve as "interior" symbols; they are, that is, recognized as symbolic by characters in the novel. Still others, largely because of the frequency with which or crucial contexts in which they appear, can be seen by the careful reader to take on symbolic significance. The "huge red transport truck" of chapter two, for example, can be seen as a sort of epitome of the mechanical-industrial economy—the bigness, the newness, the mobility, the massive efficiency, even the inhumanity (*No Riders*) and lack of trust—"a brass padlock stood straight out from the hasp on the big back doors" (p. 8). It is a mobile era in which one must accommodate to the mass mechanization in order to survive. Farmers can no longer hope to get by with a team and a wagon. And Steinbeck finds in the used-car business (chapter seven), preying on the need to move out and move quickly, an apt representation for the exploitation of those who have not yet been able to accommodate: "In the towns, on the edges of the towns, in fields, in vacant lots, the used-car yards, the wreckers' yards, the garages with blazoned signs—Used Cars, Good Used Cars, Cheap transportation" (p. 83). The Joads' makeshift truck aptly represents their predicament—their need to move, their inability to move efficiently or in style, their over-all precariousness: "The engine was noisy, full of little clashings, and the brake rods banged. There was a wooden creaking from the wheels, and a thin jet of steam escaped through a hole in the top of the radiator cap" (p. 133).[5] Steinbeck makes overt the symbolic nature of this truck; when the members of the family meet for their final council before migrating, they meet near the truck: "The house was dead, and the fields were dead; but this truck was the active thing, the living principle" (p. 135). Here, as throughout the novel, the Joads' predicament is a representative instance of the predicaments of thousands. Highway 66 is the "main migrant road" (chapter twelve), and on this "long concrete path" move the dispossessed, the "people in flight": "In the day ancient leaky radiators sent up columns of steam, loose connecting rods hammered and pounded. And the men driving the trucks and the overloaded cars listened apprehensively. How far between towns? It is a terror between towns. If something breaks—well, if something breaks we camp right here while Jim walks to town and gets a part and walks back" (p. 161). Along this route the dispossessed farmers find that they are not alone in their troubles. The independent, small-scale service station operator is being squeezed out of his livelihood just as the farmers have been; Tom tells the poor operator that he too will soon be a part of the vast moving (p. 174). And the various types of vehicles moving along Route 66 are obvious status symbols. Some have "class an' speed"; these are the insolent chariots of the exploiters. Others are the beat-up, overloaded conveyors of

---

[5] Of course it is inevitable that the poor condition of the Joads' truck parallels their own predicament; they cannot afford anything better. But the point is that the truck becomes so accurate an index that the author can use it for metonomic expression of the owners' plight; deterioration of the truck expresses deterioration of the family. A symbol is not the less a symbol because it functions well at the literal level.

the exploited in search of a better life. The reactions of those who are better-off to the sad vehicles of the Okies are representative of their lack of understanding and sympathy:

> "Jesus, I'd hate to start out in a jalopy like that."
> "Well, you and me got sense. Them goddamn Okies got no sense and no feeling. They ain't human. A human being wouldn't live like they do. A human being couldn't stand it to be so dirty and miserable. They ain't a hell of a lot better than gorillas." (p. 301)

The Okies are conscious of vehicles as status symbols and automatically distrust anyone in a better car. When a new Chevrolet pulls into the laborers' camp, the laborers automatically know that it brings trouble. Similarly the condition of the Okies' vehicles provides perfect parallels for their own sad state. As the Joads are trying to move ahead without being able to ascertain exactly where they are headed—"even if we got to crawl"—so their truck's "dim lights felt along the broad black highway ahead" (p. 384). As the Joads' condition worsens, so naturally does that of their truck (e.g., "the right head light blinked on and off from a bad connection"— p. 548). In the development of the novel their vehicles are so closely identified with the Okies that a statement of some damage to the vehicles becomes obviously symbolic of other troubles for the owners. When the disastrous rains come, "beside the tents the old cars stood, and water fouled the ignition wires and water fouled the carburetors" (p. 590). The disastrousness of the ensuing flood is quite clearly signaled by mention of the "trucks and automobiles deep in the slowly moving water" (p. 614).

As the Okies' vehicles provide an accurate index to their circumstances, so do the animals they own, particularly their pets. The deserted cat that Tom and Casy find when they survey the Joads' deserted farm represents the forlorn state of the dispossessed (see pp. 57–60—the cat actually foreshadows the appearance of Muley Graves with his tales of lonely scavengering). The dogs that appear when Tom and Casy reach Uncle John's place are indicative of human behavior in the face of new circumstances (one sniffs cautiously up to examine the strangers, while the other seeks some adequate excuse for avoiding the possible danger—p. 98). After the company's tractors move in and the share-croppers are "shoved off" their land, the pets that they left behind must fend for themselves and thus gradually revert to the primitive state of their ancestors—a reversion not unlike the desperate measures that the Okies are driven to by adversity and animosity: "The wild cats crept in from the fields at night, but they did not mew at the doorstep any more. They moved like shadows of a cloud across the moon, into the rooms to hunt the mice" (p. 159). The Joads take a dog with them on their flight to California, but he is not prepared to adjust to the new, fast, mechanized life thrust upon him; when his owners stop for gas and water, he wanders out to the great highway—"A big swift car whisked near, tires squealed. The dog dodged helplessly, and with a shriek, cut off in the middle, went under the wheels" (p. 177). The owner of the dilapidated independent service station comments on the sad scene, "A dog jus' don' last no time near a highway. I had three dogs run over in a year. Don't keep none, no more" (p. 177). After the Joads have been in California for a while and discover the grim facts of life for them there, they move on to another "Hooverville" camp of migrants. They find their fellow job-seekers hungry, fearful, and distrustful; the single pet there vividly expresses the general attitude or atmosphere of the place: "A lean brown mongrel dog came sniffing around the side of the tent. He was nervous and flexed to run. He sniffed close before he was aware of the two men, and then looking up he saw them, leaped sideways, and fled, ears back, bony tail clamped protectively" (p. 341). Yet having pets is indicative of the love and sympathy of which man is capable when in favorable circumstances. The simple, "natural" Joads never lose their appreciation for pets. When their fortunes are at their lowest ebb, Ma still holds hopes for a pleasant future: " 'Wisht we had a dog,' Ruthie said. [Ma replied] 'We'll have a dog; have a cat too' " (p. 596).

Pets, then, serve as symbolic indices to human situations; and other animal symbols are used to excellent advantage. One of Steinbeck's favorite devices is the use of epitome—the description of some object or event, apart from the main movement of the narrative, which symbolically sums up something central to the meaning of the narrative. Toward the end of *The Grapes of Wrath* the migrants are gathered about a fire, telling stories, and one of them recounts an experience of a single Indian brave whom they were forced to shoot—epitomizing the indomitability and dignity of man, and foreshadowing Casy's fate.[6]

---

[6]"They was a brave on a ridge, against the sun. Knowed he stood out. Spread his arms an' stood." Finally the soldiers are prevailed upon to shoot him down. "An' he wasn' big—he'd looked so grand—up there. All tore to pieces an' little. Ever see a cock pheasant, stiff and beautiful, ever' feather drawed an' painted, an'

We have already noted the use of animals for symbolic foreshadowing (for instance, the dispossessed cat and Muley Graves).[7] Probably Steinbeck's most famous use of the symbolic epitome is the land turtle.[8] The progress of the Okies, representative of the perseverance of "Manself," is neatly foreshadowed in the description of the turtle's persistent forward movement: he slowly plods his way, seeking to prevail in the face of adversities, and he succeeds in spite of insects, such obstacles as the highway, motorists' swerving to hit him (though some swerve to avoid hitting him), Tom's imprisoning him for awhile in his coat, the attacks of a cat, and so on. Steinbeck does not leave discernment of the rich parallels wholly to the reader's imagination. There are, for instance, similarities between Tom's progress along the dirt road and the turtle's: "And as the turtle crawled on down the embankment, its shell dragged dirt over the seeds . . . drawing a wavy shallow trench in the dust with its shell" (p. 22); and "Joad plodded along, dragging his cloud of dust behind him . . . dragging his heels a little in the dust" (p. 24—at this point in the novel Tom has not yet begun to sow the seeds of new growth among the downtrodden Okies). Casy remarks on the indomitability of the turtle, and its similarity to himself: "Nobody can't keep a turtle though. They work at it and work at it, and at last one day they get out and away they go—off somewheres. It's like me" (p. 28). But at this point in the novel Casy is not altogether like the turtle, for he has not yet discovered the goal to which he will devote himself unstintingly: " 'Goin' someplace,' he repeated. 'That's right, he's goin' someplace. Me—I don't know where I'm goin' ' " (p. 29).[9]

---

even his eyes drawed in pretty? An' bang! You pick him up—bloody an' twisted, an' you spoiled somepin better'n you; . . . you spoiled somepin in yaself, an' you can't never fix it up" (p. 445).

[7]There are in *Grapes* numerous instances of foreshadowing which do not participate in either of the dominant motifs. For example, Rose of Sharon's gesture of human sharing at the end of the novel is foreshadowed in Tom's first meal in the government camp: a mother breast-feeding her child invites him to share the breakfast she is cooking (p. 395).

[8]Kenneth Burke has called the turtle a "mediating material object for tying together Tom, Casy, and the plot, a kind of externalizing vessel, or 'symbol' "— see *The Philosophy of Literary Form* (New York, 1957), pp. 68–69.

[9]The case of the turtle is an excellent example of the intricate interrelationships of the Joads' story and the interchapters (i.e., those which do not deal directly with the Joad plot). All of chapter three is devoted to description of the turtle's slow, apparently unwitting but nonetheless definite progress. Yet, under

Animal epitomes, such as the turtle and the "lean gray cat," occur several times at crucial points. And frequently a person's character will be represented by his reaction to or treatment of lower animals. As Tom and Casy walk along the dusty road a gopher snake wriggles across their path; Tom peers at it, sees that it is harmless, and says, " 'Let him go' " (p. 93). Tom is not cruel or vicious, but he does recognize the need to prevent or put down impending disaster. Later, a "rattlesnake crawled across the road and Tom hit it and broke it and left it squirming" (p. 314). The exploitation of the Okies is symbolized by the grossly unfair price paid a share-cropper for the matched pair of bay horses he is forced to sell. In this purchase of the bays, the exploiters are buying a part of the croppers' history, their loves and labors; and a swelling bitterness is part of the bargain: "You're buying years of work, toil in the sun; you're buying a sorrow that can't talk. But watch it, mister" (p. 118).

Animals convey symbolic significance throughout the novel. When the Okies are about to set out on what they are aware will be no pleasure jaunt to California—though they scarcely have any idea how dire will be the journey and the life at the end of it—an ominous "shadow of a buzzard slid across the earth, and the family all looked up at the sailing black bird" (p. 227). In the light of the more obvious uses of animals as epitomes or omens, it is easy to see that other references to animals, which might otherwise seem incidental, are intentionally parallel to the actions or troubles of people. Here is a vivid parallel for the plight of the share-cropper, caught in the vast, rapid, mechanized movement of the industrial economy (the great highway is persistently the bearer of symbolic phenomena):

> A jackrabbit got caught in the lights and he bounced along ahead, cruising easily, his great ears flopping with every jump. Now and then he tried to break off the road, but the wall of darkness thrust him back. Far ahead bright headlights appeared and bore down on them. The rabbit hesitated, faltered, then turned and bolted toward the lesser lights of the Dodge. There was a small soft jolt as he went under the wheels. The oncoming car swished by. (p. 252)

As the weary Okies gather in a Hooverville to try to find some way out of the disaster they have flown into, moths circle frantically

---

analysis this chapter, like that on the used-car lots, for instance, proves to be an integral part of the "symbolic structure" of the novel.

about the single light: "A lamp bug slammed into the lantern and broke itself, and fell into darkness" (p. 255). While the wary mongrel at the camp represents the timorous doubts of the Okies, the arrogant skunks that prowl about at night are reminiscent of the imperious deputies and owners who intimidate the campers. The Okies are driven like animals, forced to live like animals, and frequently the treatment they receive from their short-term employers is not as good as that given farm animals:

> Fella had a team of horses, had to use 'em to plow an' cultivate an' mow, wouldn' think a turnin' 'em out to starve when they wasn't workin'.
> Them's horses—we're men. (p. 592)

We have seen that both machines and animals serve as effective symbolic devices in *The Grapes of Wrath*. Frequently the machine and animal motifs are conjoined to afford a doubly rich imagery or symbolism. Thus the banks are seen as monstrous animals, but *mechanical* monsters: "the banks were machines and masters all at the same time" (p. 43). The men for whom the share-croppers formerly worked disclaim responsibility: "It's the monster. The bank isn't like a man" (p. 45). The tractors that the banks send in are similarly monstrous—"snub-nosed monsters, raising the dust and sticking their snouts into it, straight down into the country, across the country, through fences, through dooryards, in and out of gullies in straight lines" (p. 47). And the man driving the tractor is no longer a man; he is "a part of the monster, a robot in the seat" (p. 48). Their inability to stop these monsters represents the frantic frustration of the dispossessed; Grampa Joad tries to shoot a tractor, and does get one of its headlights, but the monster keeps on moving across their land (p. 62). The new kind of mechanical farming is contrasted with the old kind of personal contact with the land. The new kind is easy and efficient. "So easy that the wonder goes out of work, so efficient that the wonder goes out of land and the working of it, and with the wonder the deep understanding and the relation" (p. 157).

We have seen that machines are usually instruments or indices of misfortune in Steinbeck's novel. But to assume that machinery is automatically or necessarily bad for Steinbeck would be a serious mistake. Machines are *instruments*, and in the hands of the right people they can be instruments of good fortune. When the turtle tries to cross the highway, one driver tries to smash him,

while another swerves to miss him (p. 22);[10] it depends on who is
behind the wheel. Al's relationship with the truck is indicative of
the complex problems of accommodating in a machine age. He
knows about motors, so he can take care of the truck and put it to
good use. He is admitted to a place of responsibility in the family
council because of his up-to-date ability. He becomes "the soul of
the car" (p. 167). The young people are more in tune with the
machines of their times, whereas the older ones are not prepared
to accommodate to the exigencies of the industrial economy:

> Casy turned to Tom. "Funny how you fellas can fix a car. Jus'
> light right in an' fix her. I couldn't fix no car, not even now when I
> seen you do it."
> "Got to grow into her when you're a little kid," Tom said. "It
> ain't jus' knowin'. It's more'n that. Kids now can tear down a car
> 'thout even thinkin' about it." (p. 252)

The tractors that shove the croppers off their land are not inherently evil; they are simply the symptoms of unfair exploitation.
In one of the interchapters (fourteen) Steinbeck expresses the
thought that the machines are in themselves of neutral value:

> Is a tractor bad? Is the power that turns the long furrows wrong? If
> this tractor were ours it would be good—not mine, but ours. If our
> tractor turned the long furrows of our land, it would be good. Not
> my land, but ours. We could love that tractor then as we have loved
> this land when it was ours. But this tractor does two things—it turns
> the land and turns us off the land. There is little difference between
> this tractor and a tank. The people are driven, intimidated, hurt by
> both. (pp. 205–206)

Machinery, like the science and technology that can develop
bigger and better crops (see pp. 473–77), is not enough for
progress; there must be human understanding and cooperation.
The Okies—through a fault not really their own—have been
unable to adjust to the machinery of industrialization. Toward the
very last of the novel Ma pleads with Al not to desert the family,
because he is the only one left qualified to handle the truck that
has become so necessary a part of their lives. As the flood creeps
up about the Joads, the truck is inundated, put out of action. But

---

[10]Steinbeck makes frequent use of such contrasts or juxtapositions. The
cheerfulness of the Saturday night dance at the government camp, for example, is
effectively juxtaposed with the harsh grumblings of the hyper-religious campers
who do not attend (p. 450).

the novel ends on a hopeful note of human sharing, and we may surmise that the Okies (or at least their children) can eventually assimilate themselves into a machine-oriented society.

Some critics have noted Steinbeck's preoccupation with animal images and symbols, and labeled his view of man as "biological."[11] This label is a gross oversimplification, responsible for a good deal of misreading of Steinbeck's work. The animal motif in *Grapes* does not at all indicate that man is or ought to be exactly like the lower animals. The Okies crawl across the country like ants, live like pigs, and fight amongst themselves like cats, mainly because they have been forced into this animalistic existence. Man can plod on in his progress like the turtle, but he can also become conscious of his goals and deliberately employ new devices in attaining those goals. Man's progress need not be blind; for he can couple human knowledge with human love, and manipulate science and technology to make possible the betterment of himself and all his fellows. Steinbeck does not present a picture of utopia in his novel, but the dominant motifs do indicate that such a society is possible.

It has been a fundamental assumption of this study that dominant motifs are of central importance in the form and meaning of certain works of fiction. In this particular case we would contend that Steinbeck's intricate and masterful manipulation of the various references to machines and animals is an essential factor in the stature of *The Grapes of Wrath* as one of the monuments of twentieth-century American literature. By their very pervasiveness— the recurrence of the components that constitute the motifs—the references contribute significantly to the unity of the work; they help, for instance, to bind together the Joad chapters with those which generalize the meaning that the Joads' story illustrates. Certain animals and machines play important parts on the literal level of the story, and these and others serve to underscore principal developments or "themes" in the novel. Certain animals and machines are recognizably symbolic within the context of the

[11]See, e.g., Edmund Wilson, "The Boys in the Back Room [5. John Steinbeck]," *A Literary Chronicle: 1920–1950* (New York, 1956), pp. 230–39. Peter Lisca (*The Wide World of John Steinbeck*) has tried to dispel this misconception of Steinbeck's biologism—as has Frederick Bracher, "Steinbeck and the Biological View of Man," in Tedlock and Wicker, pp. 183–96. While there are still those who prefer to view *Grapes* as a primarily sociological document, the oversimplification of Steinbeck's "biological view" has been pretty well quashed in recent criticism.

story, and still others (the epitomes for example) can be discerned as much more meaningful than their overt, apparently incidental mention might at first seem to indicate. Both the interior and the more subtle symbols—as reinforced by the recurrence of related allusions or figures of speech—are interwoven and played off against one another to such an extent that the overall meaning is not merely made more vivid: it is considerably enriched. A consideration of these motifs does not begin to exhaust the richness of the book; but this discussion can, we hope, contribute to a fuller understanding of Steinbeck's novel as a consummate complex work of art.

Agrarianism and Technology
in Steinbeck's
The Grapes of Wrath

by Horst Groene

It is commonly acknowledged that traditional American modes of thinking can be observed in John Steinbeck's *The Grapes of Wrath*. With their journey to California, the Joad family follow the example set by the pioneers who left the disagreeable conditions in their home states and looked for the fulfilment of the American dream in the rich opportunities of the West.[1] Like the pioneers the Joads still believe in the prospects of the frontier and hope to acquire a small piece of land, which they can till with their own hands. In their visions of a boundless fecundity with which California is blessed, they revive what Henry Nash Smith has called "the myth of the garden": the old dream of an agricultural paradise in the West, which is here transferred from the Mississippi Valley to the fertile land of California.[2]

These ideas reveal the strong influence of agrarian thinking, which can be traced back to Benjamin Franklin, J. Hector St. John de Crèvecoeur, and especially to Thomas Jefferson, who gave it classic expression in Query XIX of his *Notes on Virginia (1784–85)*.[3] Like Jefferson and his nineteenth century followers, Steinbeck favours the widespread ownership of land holdings and believes in

"Agrarianism and Technology in Steinbeck's *The Grapes of Wrath*" by Horst Groene. From *Southern Review*, 9, 1 (1976), 27–31. Reprinted by permission of the editor and the author.

[1]Cf. Thomas R. Goethals, *The Grapes of Wrath: A Critical Commentary* (New York: American R.D.M. Corporation, 1963), pp. 19–20.

[2]Henry Nash Smith, *Virgin Land: The American West as Symbol and Myth* (Cambridge: Harvard University Press, 2nd ed., 1970), pp. 123–132.

[3]Cf. ibid., pp. 125–128 and Leo Marx, *The Machine in the Garden: Technology and the Pastoral Ideal in America* (New York: Oxford University Press, 1964), pp. 122–130.

the dignity and virtue of the independent farmer who can live by the fruits of his labour and is nobody's servant.[4] In his support of small scale farming, he was also influenced by the back-to-the-soil movement, which found so many adherents for its programme of *Five Acres and Independence*[5] in the Depression Era.

The impact of the ideal figure of the Western yeoman farmer is also discernible in the characterization of the Joads and other tenant farmers, who, regardless of their coarse and unrefined speech and manners, appear basically good and virtuous.[6] They are portrayed as generous and helpful people, adhering to their moral code, displaying considerable strength of character in the face of constant adversity and preserving their dignity in spite of growing hostility. Through his sympathetic treatment of the Joads and other dispossessed farmers, Steinbeck has created a more appealing picture of the Western farmer and his plight than did his nineteenth century forerunners Joseph Kirkland, E. W. Howe and Hamlin Garland.

Steinbeck's agrarian ideals apparently made him also resent the mechanization and industrialization of agriculture with its concomitant absentee ownership. In *The Grapes of Wrath* machines destroy the close bond between Man and Nature, make the tenant farmer redundant and force him off the land so that he becomes a shiftless migrant worker. It is above all the tractor which threatens the self-sufficient and satisfying way of life of the small farmer and which becomes something approaching a new symbol of the traditional "anti-pastoral counterforce of industrialism," which Leo Marx has described with such wealth of detail in his investigation of the impact of modern technology on American thinking.[7]

Nevertheless, nineteenth century ideals could not provide adequate solutions to the problems posed by the agricultural revolution. Steinbeck, too, had to acknowledge this at the end of

---

[4]Cf. Chester E. Eisinger, "Jeffersonian Agrarianism in *The Grapes of Wrath*," *University of Kansas City Review*, XIV (Winter, 1947), 149–154.

[5]Title of the popular book by Maurice G. Kains, published 1935, 2nd ed. 1943; for details cf. Warren French, "A Troubled Nation—'How Nice It's Gonna Be, Maybe, In California,'" in *The Social Novel at the End of an Era* (Carbondale and Edwardsville: Southern Illinois University Press, 1966), pp. 42–86.

[6]For the idealized figure of the Western yeoman farmer cf. Smith, *Virgin Land*, pp. 126–130.

[7]Cf. *The Machine in the Garden*, pp. 24–27.

his novel—in spite of his agrarian predilections. For in California the Joads are soon confronted with the situation that half a century before prompted Frederick Jackson Turner to write his great essay "The Significance of the Frontier in American History" (1893): the frontier is closed, the dream of owning a small piece of land must be buried as wishful thinking. Even worse, living conditions deteriorate all the time and the family slowly dissolves in spite of Ma Joad's efforts. Tom, their leader, who feels such strong attachment to the soil, is forced to flee, and the novel ends with the remnants of the Joad Clan trying to survive the flood-like rains in the box car and barn. True, critics are agreed that *The Grapes of Wrath* ends on a somewhat optimistic note: Rose of Sharon's gesture of help can be understood as a sign of the indestructible life force of the people.[8] But it is undeniable that such an interpretation has to rely heavily on the symbolic aspects of this conclusion, whereas on the level of concrete action the Joads' situation is quite hopeless.

There are, however, some indications that Steinbeck not only concedes the impossibility of realizing agrarian concepts, but that he also begins to accept the opportunities offered by modern industrial society as a possible solution to the migrant worker's problems. One point is the shift in attitude toward the application of modern technology in agriculture which occurs between chapters 5 and 25. True, a major topic of chapter 5 is the criticism of absentee ownership and of the unscrupulous methods of the banks. At the same time, however, the use of machinery in agriculture is strongly condemned: machines sever the emotional bond between Man and Nature, which can only exist where farmers till the soil with their own hands. It is particularly the imagery which betrays Steinbeck's distrust of mechanization in agriculture. The tractors with their ploughing and sowing implements are likened to insects and monsters raping the land. They corrupt the drivers, who become their slaves and act like robots without a will of their own.

> The tractors came over the roads and into the fields, great crawlers, moving like insects, having the incredible strength of insects. . . .

[8]Cf. Theodore Pollock, "On the Ending of *The Grapes of Wrath*," *Modern Fiction Studies,* IV (1958), 177–78; F. W. Watt, *Steinbeck* (Edinburgh: Oliver and Boyd, 1962), p. 74; Jules Chametzky, "The Ambivalent Endings of *The Grapes of Wrath*," *Modern Fiction Studies*, XI (1965), 34–35; Tetsumaro Hayashi, "Women and the Principle of Continuity in *The Grapes of Wrath*," *Kyushu American Literature,* X (1967), 75–80.

> Snub-nosed monsters, raising the dust and sticking their snouts into it, straight down the country, across the country, through fences, through dooryards, in and out of gullies in straight lines. . . . The man sitting in the iron seat did not look like a man: gloved, goggled, rubber dust-mask over nose and mouth, he was a part of the monster, a robot in the seat.[9]

In chapter 25, however, Steinbeck lauds the achievements of chemistry, experimental farming, and modern technology in agriculture. The highest praise again goes to the men who work with their own hands grafting the fruit trees. But the dichotomy between people who have direct contact with soil and plants and those who work in the laboratory or use machines is no longer maintained. The cultivators are now described as beneficial implements which help to increase fertility:

> Along the rows the cultivators move, tearing the spring grass and turning it under to make a fertile earth, breaking the ground to hold the water up near the surface, ridging the ground in little pools for the irrigation, destroying the weed roots that may drink the water away from the trees. (p. 318)

This praise of technological progress in agriculture serves to heighten the accusation of deliberate waste of agricultural goods in California. But at the same time it is a clear indication of Steinbeck's realization that undeniable advantages can be gained for the population at large by applying modern technology to agriculture.

These ideas expressed in chapter 25 could be considered as an isolated phenomenon without further relevance to the line of thought in the novel, were they not supported by an interesting development in the constellation of the characters. When the former male leader Tom Joad, who feels so strongly attached to the soil, is forced to leave the family, his position is taken over by Al Joad, the mechanic, who has no interest in agriculture and dreams of working in a garage in the city. Decidedly a minor figure in the early parts of the novel, he constantly gains in stature and maturity during the wanderings in California.

At the beginning, Al is introduced as a "smart aleck" and a "randy boy" who spends most of his time chasing girls. He is a good mechanic and has bought a usable car for the trip to California, but has delayed making the necessary improvements because of his time-consuming adventures with girls. He does not

---

[9]John Steinbeck, *The Grapes of Wrath*, Penguin Modern Classics (Harmondsworth, 15th repr., 1971), pp. 33 f. All quotations refer to this edition.

object to playing the role of the little brother to Tom, whom he admires and whose orders he willingly obeys. And though he is admitted to the family council, he is only consulted in matters concerning the truck (chap. 8, pp. 76 ff., chap. 10, pp. 87 ff.). On the trip along route 66 no significant development is yet discernible. Al is a competent mechanic and a conscientious driver, who is not really to blame for the burning out of the connecting-rod and the break-down of the car. It is in California, then, where those changes occur which make him a leading member of the family.

Al begins to act independently and shows circumspection and foresight when he secretly keeps back a barrel of petrol so that the family can leave the government camp (pp. 321–22). Without asking his father's and uncle's permission he picks up a man from the camp and decides to return there because their search for work is futile (pp. 292–93). He keeps his head and thinks up a clever excuse for Tom's disappearance when the guards at the Hooper ranch have to be deceived in order to save his brother's life. He is also able to procure the petrol necessary to drive north (pp. 368–69). Finally, when Tom is forced to hide, it is he, and not Pa Joad or Uncle John, who becomes his mother's main support. He takes care of the car as best he can, and tries, though in vain, to save it from the rising water (pp. 399, 405–06). He defends his father against an enraged man who wants to beat him up (p. 407), and it is he who proposes to build a platform in the box car from the sideboards of the truck (pp. 408–09). Also, instead of continuing to chase girls, he himself decides to get married to Aggie Wainwright (p. 389) so that the insinuations that Ma Joad and Mrs. Wainwright had planned to make are no longer necessary.

The clearest sign, however, that he is acting responsibly is his willingness to help his family. He is not overjoyed at staying with them, because he is determined to look for a job in the city. But unlike Connie Rivers, who deserts his pregnant wife when things get really bad, he remains with his people and supports them as best as he can until he is left behind in the box car to look after the truck. Connie Rivers, too, is attracted by the idea of making a living in the city and actually puts this notion into Al's head (p. 167), but he is a weakling who just talks about studying books at night and becoming an electrician. With Al, however, we can be sure that he will make his way in the city, for he has already proved himself a competent mechanic and a responsible man on several occasions.

Thus a further thread is discernible in the complex texture of the ending of *The Grapes of Wrath*. The Joads' hopes of owning a small piece of land are shattered, and worse than that, their attempts to subsist as migrant workers have failed. From their bitter experiences they have learned that the solidarity of all oppressed people is more important than loyalty to the family and that joint actions of all the migrant workers are the only means of improving their living and working conditions.[10] But a concrete solution is not in sight so that Steinbeck has to resort to his symbolic conclusion in order to avoid complete pessimism.

A practical way out is suggested, however, in the figure of Al Joad. He no longer believes in making a living as a farmer, but looks to the city and the chances offered there.[11] The frontier does not influence his thoughts; he trusts in making headway by staking his claims at the frontier of opportunity. Though he does not aim at becoming a millionaire like Henry Ford, he is confident that he can earn a decent wage as a mechanic. The further developments in California proved that only such a move to the city could alleviate the miserable living conditions of the "Okies." The Second World War provided sufficient jobs in the industries of San Francisco and other industrialized locations.[12] Thus, by placing Al Joad increasingly in the foreground and by conceding in chapter 25 the advantages to be gained from applying modern technology to agriculture, Steinbeck qualifies his one-sided agrarianism and begins to accept the positive aspects of mechanization and industrialization. Even though his almost mystic love of nature makes Steinbeck tend to retain nineteenth century ideals, he is not so backward and old-fashioned as some critics suspect him of being.[13]

[10]Cf. Peter Lisca, *The Wide World of John Steinbeck* (New Brunswick, N.J.: Rutgers University Press, 1958, 6th repr., 1969), pp. 176–77; Warren French, *John Steinbeck* (New Haven: Twayne Publishers, 1961), pp. 106–08; Joseph Fontenrose, *John Steinbeck: An Introduction and Interpretation* (New York: Barnes and Noble, 1963), p. 69.

[11]Steinbeck's fondness for cars and his admiration for skilful mechanics—Tom is another example—made it easier for him to transform Al into a major figure; cf. Walter Rundell, Jr., "Steinbeck's Image of the West," *The American West,* I (1964), 16.

[12]Cf. Fontenrose, *John Steinbeck*, p. 83.

[13]Cf. e.g. Eisinger, "Jeffersonian Agrarianism," 149, 154; Rundell, "Steinbeck's Image of the West," 6.

Mother Earth
and Earth Mother:
The Recasting of Myth
in Steinbeck's
The Grapes of Wrath

by Joan Hedrick

From Jefferson's yeoman farmer to Turner's frontier thesis, the ideology of the American dream has been closely tied to the image of an abundant, tillable soil. In this strain of historiography, the rich Western lands are a "safety valve" important to the preservation of democracy. Disgruntled New Englanders could leave behind the rock soil—and, more importantly, the social and economic changes that followed upon urbanization, immigration, and the rise of the factory—by moving West. For many who did not remove, the Western lands kept alive the myth of the garden, a land so fruitful that there was enough for all. In this way, the vast expanse of open land operated in the American imagination to keep political questions muted. As long as there was enough for everyone, it was simpler to go to a richer land than to argue with one's employer about what was a fair share or a fair day's work. Of course, this did not keep American workers from entering into frequent and often violent disputes with their employers on just these questions; but insofar as the ideology of American abundance kept such political consciousness from developing, it was tied to the myth of inexhaustible land.

In *The Grapes of Wrath*, Steinbeck aims all of his artillery at this myth in order to blast it out of the American imagination and replace it with a more political understanding. In the opening chapter, the garden of the West has turned to dust.

> In the morning the dust hung like fog, and the sun was as red as ripe new blood. All day the dust sifted down from the sky, and the next day it sifted down. An even blanket covered the earth.[1]

Factory farming methods have destroyed the topsoil and rendered the earth sterile. And even an abundant harvest is not sufficient, Steinbeck's story makes clear, as long as corporations own millions of acres and the people have the use of none. This is knowledge that Steinbeck's characters reach only after long and painful experience; their exodus to California is motivated by stock images of the garden of plenty. After the Joads reach California and understand that thousands of migrants have responded to the flyers asking for fruit pickers, just as thousands of European immigrants responded to similar flyers from American employers and shipping companies in the nineteenth century, the story becomes increasingly focused on political activity: the people's committees in the government camps, the fruit pickers' strike, Tom Joad's decision to follow in Casy's footsteps by becoming a labor organizer. But though Steinbeck succeeds in replacing the myth of the garden with self-conscious political activity, he inadvertently invokes another myth that undercuts the political thrust of his story.

Steinbeck's recasting of myth is given powerful emphasis by the structure of the book, which opens with the image of the dry, desolate land and closes with that of the nurturant, milk-producing woman. When Rose of Sharon feeds a starving man with milk from her breast, we are doubtless supposed to feel the resilience, hope, and strength that Steinbeck attributed to people like the Joads and, in particular, to Ma Joad. But this act also suggests the superfluousness of political activity: if mother earth has given out, ·one can still return to that original fount of plenty, the mother's breast.[2] This scene makes explicit the role that Ma Joad has played

---

[1]John Steinbeck, *The Grapes of Wrath* (New York: Viking Press, 1939), p. 6. Subsequent references to this edition are given parenthetically in the text.

[2]My analysis has been influenced by Dorothy Dinnerstein, *The Mermaid and the Minotaur: Sexual Arrangements and Human Malaise* (New York: Harper and Row, Publishers, 1977). Dinnerstein points out the easy transference we make between Mother Earth and Earth Mother: "Inextricable from the notion that nature is our semi-sentient early mother is the notion that she is inherently inexhaustible, that if she does not provide everything we would like to have it is because she does not

throughout the story. In death, deprivation, and uncertainty, Ma is the rock that gives the family strength.

> Her hazel eyes seemed to have experienced all possible tragedy and to have mounted pain and suffering like steps into a high calm and a superhuman understanding. She seemed to know, to accept, to welcome her position, the citadel of the family, the strong place that could not be taken. And since old Tom and the children could not know hurt or fear unless she acknowledged hurt and fear, she had practiced denying them in herself. . . . From her position as healer, her hands had grown sure and cool and quiet; and from her position as arbiter she had become remote and faultless in judgment as a goddess. (P. 108).

This is an accurate description of the way children view that seemingly all-competent woman who is their first caretaker. It is emphatically not a realistic portrait of a woman. Yet not once do Ma Joad's actions belie this childlike vision of her as a goddess. Not once does she break, or show any danger of breaking. Since she is the spokesperson for family unity, one might expect her to give some sign of weakness as, one by one, the family disappears: Grampa and Granma die, Noah and Connie wander off, Al forms a new family, Tom becomes a fugitive, and Rose of Sharon's baby dies. Ma philosophizes over these changes but gives no sign that her inner self has been touched by them. Indeed, in Steinbeck's telling, she had no inner self.

To Steinbeck's unwavering faith in women's ability to absorb tragedy, one could compare the perspective of J. Russell Smith, who, commenting on the absence of monuments to commemorate the romance and tragedy of the Great Plains, wrote:

> A lion does not write a book, nor does the weather erect a monument at the place where the pride of a woman was broken for want of a pair of shoes, or where a man worked five years in vain to build a home and gave it up, bankrupt and whipped, or where a baby

---

want to, that her treasure is infinite and can if necessary be taken by force. This view of Mother Earth is in turn identical with the view of the Earth Mother, a bottomless source of richness, a being not human enough to have needs of an importance as primary, as self-evident, as the importance of our own needs, but voluntary and conscious enough so that if she does not give us what we expect she is withholding it on purpose and we are justified in getting it from her any way we can. The murderous infantilism of our relation to nature follows inexorably from the murderous infantilism of our sexual arrangements. To outgrow the one we must outgrow the other" (p. 110). (Quoted by permission of Harper and Row, Publishers, Inc., and the author.)

died for the want of good milk, or where the wife went insane for sheer monotony and blasted hope.[3]

Or to Steinbeck's Ma Joad, one could compare Tillie Olsen's portrait of Mazie's Mother in *Yonnondio*. Physically exhausted by the struggle to make a life for herself and her children during the thirties, she drifts into "a fog of pain that seemed the only reality."[4] The following passage describes her reaction to going through drawers of children's clothes that need mending.

> It was not that the clothes were beyond or almost beyond mending and that there were none others and no money to buy more; not that four children slept here in this closet bedroom, three on a mattress on the floor; not that in the corners dust curled in feathers, dust that was Dirt that Breeds Disease You Make Your Children Sick; not that one of her children had stood a few minutes ago (ah, which hurts more, the earlier averted face or this?) looking at her with pain and fear and pity for her in her eyes.
>
> It was not any and it was all of these things that brought her now to swaying in the middle of the floor, twisting and twisting the rompers in soundless anguish. It was that she felt so worn, so helpless; that it loomed gigantic beyond her, impossible ever to achieve, beyond, beyond any effort or doing of hers: that task of making a better life for her children to which her being was bound.[5]

I do not wish to insist that all portraits of proletarian women should show them breaking under the gigantic effort to survive; surely there is much to be said for Steinbeck's insistence on Ma Joad's strength and endurance. But to neglect to show the erosion of the human spirit that was perhaps the greatest tragedy of the Depression is unconsciously to foster the belief that woman is a bottomless well of suffering and endurance upon whom men can make drafts: from her mythic abundance, she will supply what the exhausted land cannot.

Critics have noticed Steinbeck's ploy, but only to reinforce, not criticize, the myth. "A person of common sense, stamina, and compassion," Paul McCarthy writes, "Ma symbolizes both the

[3]Dorothea Lange and Paul Shuster Taylor, *An American Exodus: A Record of Human Erosion* (New York: Reynal and Hitchcock, 1939), p. 103.

[4]Excerpted from the book *Yonnondio: From the Thirties* by Tillie Olsen, p. 71. Copyright © 1974 by Tillie Olsen. Reprinted by permission of Delacorte Press/ Seymour Lawrence.

[5]*Ibid.*, pp. 104–105.

family's strength and the eternal qualities of motherhood."⁶ To attribute Ma's strength to "the eternal qualities of motherhood" focuses attention on the childlike perceptions that are the underpinnings of myth, and obscures the real sources of Ma's strength, which Steinbeck has enough novelistic integrity to show, even if he resorts to myth to explain them. Real strength of character emanates, not from some biological or mystical quality, but from the work roles of the men and women Steinbeck portrays. A corollary to this is that individual strength is not individually created; it arises out of the social relationships from which people derive both their identity and their reason to be.

Tetsumaro Hayashi has observed that "as the men in [*The Grapes of Wrath*] grow weaker, the women become stronger."⁷ This is true on the level of generalization (I discuss later the prominent exceptions, Jim Casy and Tom Joad), but Hayashi is content to attribute this to the working out of Steinbeck's "humanistic theme," "the sense of continuity for man through the female as the Great Mother." A more precise explanation emerges in the texture of the novel. After the crops have dried up and blown away, the men have no work. "The men sat in the doorways of their houses; their hands were busy with sticks and little rocks. The men sat still—thinking—figuring" (p. 7). This idle, restless movement of the hands is the most characteristic activity of the men in *The Grapes of Wrath*. Casy "found a twig with which to draw his thoughts on the ground. He swept the leaves from a square and smoothed the dust. And he drew angles and made little circles" (p. 28). As the women watch the men figuring helplessly in the dust, they quietly move into the houses. "They knew that a man so hurt and so perplexed may turn in anger, even on people he loves." The women warn the children, "Go out and play. But don't go near your father. He might whale you if you go near him. And the women went on with the work, but all the time they watched the men squatting in the dust—perplexed and figuring" (p. 47). It is significant that "the women went on with the work." Though there are no crops to be harvested, there are clothes to mend, cornmeal to stir, side meat to cut up for dinner. In a time of unemployment, women embody continuity, not out of some mythic identity as the Great Mother, but simply because their work, being in the private

⁶Paul McCarthy, *John Steinbeck* (New York: Frederick Ungar Publishing Company, 1980), p. 74.

⁷Tetsumaro Hayashi, "Steinbeck's Women in *The Grapes of Wrath*: A New Perspective," *Kyushu American Literature,* 18 (October 1977), p. 3.

sphere of the family, has not been taken away by the "monster." Ma's perception of life as a "flow," in which setbacks are "little eddies, little waterfalls" in a great river of life that goes on in spite of them, is directly related to the texture of her work life. When Uncle John asks her how she can be sure life will go on, how she knows that life is a flow and not "jerks" that may cataclysmically signal an end, she replies " 'Hard to say. . . . Everything we do— seems to me is·aimed right at goin' on. Seems that way to me. Even gettin' hungry—even bein' sick; some die, but the rest is tougher. Jus' try to live the day, jus' the day' " (pp. 577–578). Engaged in the very immediate tasks of daily survival—the awareness and satis- faction of bodily needs—Ma Joad participates directly to produce the sustenance. of life, and out of this comes a feeling of control and optimism. The following passage epitomizes the contrasting positions of Ma and Pa Joad: "The frying pan of potatoes was hissing and spitting over the fire. Ma moved the thick slices about with a spoon. Pa sat nearby hugging his knees" (p. 371). Each day, women derive a renewed sense of purpose and energy from the life-sustaining tasks that have been declared women's work. But this strength can at any moment be used against them. When the wondering in the dust turns to rage, if it is not politically aware and directed at the "monster," it is likely to be turned against the woman whom it is the man's responsibility to support, and whose very strength mocks his helplessness. Pa, grumbling at his loss of authority, says, "Seems like it's purty near time to get out a stick" (p. 481). But domestic violence remains a threat we are not asked to consider seriously in *The Grapes of Wrath*. To emphasize a woman's economic dependence and physical vulnerability would dissolve that childlike dream of an Earth Mother, and so undercut the emotional satisfactions of Steinbeck's myth.

The Grapes of Wrath could be read as the story of the reunion of a mother and son, and their forced separation at the end. Certainly the strongest emotions the tale evokes are centered in mother- child relationships, whether it is Ma lovingly turning over in her mouth the name of her daughter, Rose of Sharon, or Ma greeting with repressed emotion the unexpected return of her son from prison. Neither father-son relationships nor relationships between lovers can match this intensity. Pa is reduced to a giggling child by the return of his son; all he can think about is playing a trick on Ma by surprising her with Tom. And sexual relationships between men and women are robbed of their potential power by reduction to a mechanical, animalistic act. Muley remembers the first time

he lay with a girl: "Me fourteen an' stampin' an' jerkin' an'
snortin' like a buck deer, randy as a billygoat" (p. 69). Tom
remembers with some affection the man he served time for killing:
"He was a nice fella. Come a-bullin' after my sister Rosasharn
when he was a little feller. No, I liked Herb" (p. 73). He also
tells of running down a whore "like she was a rabbit" after he got
out of prison (p. 233). Neither do the longer-term relationships
between men and women, as evidenced in Ma and Pa's marriage
and that of Rose of Sharon and Connie, have the deep-running
humanity that charges Ma's relationship with Tom. Both Ma and
Tom derive strength from this mother-child bond. When we first
meet Tom, he is just an ex-con in new clothes who hitches a ride
and nips from his flask. In the opening chapters there is little hint
of the strength that he displays within the family and, later, in a
larger social role. He grows in responsibility through his relationship with his mother. She leans on him and insists that he be
strong; she means for him to hold the family together and to play
an important social role (which she does not fully understand):
" 'You're spoke for' " (p. 482). It is Ma who first voices—to Tom—
the possibility of political action. " 'Tommy, I got to thinkin' an'
dreamin' an' wonderin'. They say there's a hun'erd thousand of us
shoved out. If we was all mad the same way, Tommy—they
wouldn't hunt nobody down—' " (p. 104). Just as Ma charges
Tom's life with meaning and purpose and strength, so does Tom
(and the rest of the family) give Ma the courage to be that citadel of
strength, because she knows they are counting on her. In this way
individual strength is called forth by the social relationships
through which people are defined, and the strongest of these is the
mother-child bond.

This creates problems for the men. If they are defined as *sons,*
how are they to grow up? How can they be both strong and adult?
When the men try to act grown up and responsible in relationship
to women—when they step outside the hard, male role in which
women are "rabbits," "fillies," or "the broad behind the counter"—they only succeed in looking ridiculous: Casy's pathetic guilt
over lying with girls, Uncle John's moonings about sin, Pa's guilt
over his inept delivery of his son, Noah—these do not increase the
stature of these infantile men. Pa might conceivably be strengthened by the parent-child bond, but when he is called upon to play
this role, his infantilization is only increased. When Winfield faints
from hunger and dehydration, Ma acts quickly, but Pa complains
like a greedy child.

> Pa and Uncle John and Al came into the house. Their arms were full of sticks and bits of brush. They dropped their loads by the stove. "Now what?" Pa demanded.
> "It's Winfiel'. He needs some milk."
> "Christ Awmighty! We all need stuff!"
> Ma said, "How much'd we make today?"
> "Dollar forty-two."
> "Well, you go right over'n get a can of milk for Winfiel'."
> "Now why'd he have to get sick?"
> "I don't know why, but he is. Now you git!" Pa went grumbling out the door. (P. 542)

As long as women are defined as mothers and men as sons, the infantilization of men is virtually assured.

But there are two men in the novel who transcend this role: Casy and Tom. Significantly, Casy's movement from an unemployed preacher to a labor organizer, from idleness to social purpose, is preceded by his ability to unite seemingly opposite categories like "sin" and "virtue." His decision to leave preaching is based on his realization that " 'there ain't no sin and there ain't no virtue. There's just stuff people do. It's all part of the same thing' " (p. 32). This breaking down of religious categories parallels his breaking down of gender distinctions: Ma Joad is surprised when he offers to do the "women's work" of salting down the pork, but he replies " 'It's all work. . . . They's too much of it to split it up to men's or women's work. You got stuff to do. Leave me salt the meat' " (p. 146). By becoming a labor leader, a secular preacher, Casy unites the "here" and the "hereafter."

> Casy said quietly, "I gotta see them folks that's gone out on the road. I got a feelin' I got to see them. They gonna need help no preachin' can give 'em. Hope of heaven when their lives ain't lived? Holy Sperit when their own sperit is downcast an' sad? They gonna need help. They got to live before they can afford to die." (P. 71)

Casy's breaking down of cultural categories enables him to develop an awareness of collectivity, for he overcomes the separation of the individual from the group. Tom remembers his words:

> "Says one time he went out in the wilderness to find his own soul, an' he foun' he didn' have no soul that was his'n. Says he foun' he jus' got a little piece of a great big soul. Says a wilderness an't no good, 'cause his little piece of a soul wasn't no good 'less it was with the rest, an' was whole." (P. 570)

Tom's decision to carry on Casy's work in the labor movement, even though it will probably cost him his life, is on one level a visceral reaction to his having witnessed the unprovoked violence that ended Casy's life; it is also a working out of his mother's insistence that he is "called." But to respond to this maternal sense of mission, Tom must break with his mother. The separation that she has so resisted throughout the novel now becomes necessary to the working out of her purpose for her son. She objects: " 'How'm I gonna know 'bout you? They might kill ya an' I wouldn' know. They might hurt ya. How'm I gonna know?' " Tom responds by using Casy's logic:

> [if] "a fella ain't got a soul of his own, but on'y a piece of a big one. . . . Then it don' matter. Then I'll be all aroun' in the dark. I'll be ever'where—wherever you look. Wherever they's a fight so hungry people can eat, I'll be there. Wherever they's a cop beatin' up a guy, I'll be there. If Casy knowed, why, I'll be in the way guys yell when they're mad an'—I'll be in the way kids laugh when they're hungry an' they know supper's ready. An' when our folks eat the stuff they raise an' live in the houses they build—why I'll be there. See?" (P. 572)

The Biblical rhythms are appropriate here, for Casy and Tom, in their struggles for wholeness and at-one-ness with the world, become messianic. They lay down their lives for their fellow men. This political activism gives them a way of being both grown up and strong: the son of woman becomes the son of God. Through his relationship with Ma, Tom becomes a repository of the humanistic, "survival" values that she has espoused. Moreover, he extends this nurturant role beyond the family to the family of mankind. In the tent communities that spring up along the road, the dying child of one family becomes the dying child of all, and the birth of a new baby is cause for the celebration of all. Some of the most powerful writing in *The Grapes of Wrath* occurs in the interpolated chapters, in which Steinbeck portrays the collective responses of the people to the erosion of their lives. It is Tom's work to further these collective responses. Tom thus unites male and female categories by carrying "women's" values into the public sphere.

But this leaves unresolved the role of men within the private sphere of the family. Casy, in his incarnation as labor leader, is celibate and asexual. Tom shows affection for no woman but his mother. Men can grow up, the novel seems to say, only by leaving women alone and ascending to a higher, "spiritual" plane. The final scene, in which Rose of Sharon nurses a grown man, dramatizes the dependence that overtakes men in the presence of women. And whereas earlier Steinbeck ties women's strength realistically to their work lives, here he does not see Rose of Sharon as a flesh-and-blood person. She has just delivered a baby in a tent, without benefit of medical attention; she is dizzy, unable to walk, soaked from rain, and probably feverish—to say nothing of her psychological state after the stillbirth of her child. Nevertheless, fueled only by Ma's looking deep into her eyes, Rose of Sharon lies on the floor of the barn where they have taken shelter and insists that the starving man discovered there take her breast.

> "There!" she said. "There." Her hand moved behind his head and supported it. Her fingers moved gently in his hair. She looked up and across the barn, and her lips came together and smiled mysteriously. (P. 619)

Her severe malnutrition is doubtless responsible for her baby's death, yet Steinbeck asks us to believe not only that she has a plentiful milk supply but that, in her physically weakened state, she can act with relish the part of a mysterious madonna. In this lapse from realism into myth, Steinbeck implicitly aligns himself with the hungry old man who nurses at Rose of Sharon's breast. His is only to take and be grateful, not to wonder how or why to conceive of women's bodies as corporeal and subject to pain and distress.

When the Earth Goddess reveals herself as merely mortal, the unquestioning bliss of the child/man at the breast can easily turn to rage. One critic has observed that Steinbeck portrays his women characters in one of two ways: either as a "Great Mother," and thus a symbol of continuity, as in *To a God Unknown, The Grapes of Wrath*, and *The Winter of Our Discontent*; or as "a principle of destruction and dis-continuity," as in *The Long Valley, Tortilla Flat, Of Mice and Men, Cannery Row, The Wayward Bus,* and *East of Eden.*[8] This image of woman as Goddess/Destroyer is essentially a child's myth; she is both more and less than this. The political power of *The Grapes of Wrath* lies in Steinbeck's ability to look clear-eyed at the myth of the garden of plenty; had he looked with as much realism at the myth of the earth mother, he would have written a truer, more political, and more humanistic book.

[8]*Ibid.,* p. 1.

The Picaresque Saint

by R.W.B. Lewis

In the figure of Tom Joad, in *The Grapes of Wrath*, Steinbeck offers an illuminating example of what I have been calling the picaresque saint. It might therefore be sensibly argued that an entire chapter should be devoted to Steinbeck. But there is a distinct unevenness in his work, and a certain failure of artistic promise. Steinbeck can more fittingly appear here as a link between writers as seemingly remote from one another as Silone and Faulkner, a link that helps us see more clearly the essential pattern of second generation fiction. If Steinbeck has not provided original and enduring treatments of major themes, he offers a very valuable perspective on those writers who have.

Between Steinbeck and Silone, one observes a lengthily unfolding analogy that changes at last into a marked difference. The two men were born in the same year (1900) [a glance at the *Chronology of Important Dates* on page 150 will show that Steinbeck's year of birth is actually 1902—*Ed.*], and in their first fictional writings, about three decades later, both men chose to deal with primitive penniless persons—the cheerful California unregenerates of Tortilla Flat and the rugged Abruzzese analphabets of Fontamara. Steinbeck and Silone alike regarded these folk with affectionate humor; they chose them as their companions, as against the "civilized" and law-abiding people in the distant citified society. When hard times came—the depression in America, the congealing of the Fascist movement in Italy—both writers again chose the wretched and the victimized as companions and as the models for their fiction; both examined the situation local to them in terms of a poetry flavored with Marxism; and both articulated dramatically the immediate need to unite—to organize—to

"The Picaresque Saint." From *The Picaresque Saint* by R.W.B. Lewis (New York: J. B. Lippincott, 1958), pp. 181–86. Copyright 1956, 1958 by R.W.B. Lewis. Reprinted by permission of Harper & Row, Publishers, Inc.

rally together and strike back. This was the point reached by Steinbeck in his severely naturalistic novel *In Dubious Battle* and by Silone at the conclusion of *Fontamara* and the beginning of *Bread and Wine*. In Steinbeck's case, the problem was not new. He had always been interested in the nature of human unity, in the formation and decay of social units: even through the haze of legend that he wrapped around the episodes of *Tortilla Flat* (1935), we glimpse the rise and fall of a tiny social entity—its creation ("How Danny's Friends swore comradeship"), the challenge to it ("How the poison of possessions wrought with Pilon"), its disintegration ("How each friend departed alone"). But that was all good chivalric fun, in the mock-epic spirit. *In Dubious Battle* (1936) confronts the problem without laughter, and, with some reservations, commits itself to group activity as the only instrument of survival amidst the murderous forces of greed.

One character in the novel, to be sure, voices some of the doubts hinted at in the title. Doc Burton, a non-Communist sympathizer, tells the organizers and strikers to whom he ministers that they are "group-men," a new kind of being, something potent but also distinctly dubious. "A man in a group isn't himself at all, he's a cell in an organism that isn't like him any more than the cells in your body are like you," he says to the radical leader. The latter replies irritably that Doc Burton simply doesn't "believe in the cause"; and Doc agrees: "I don't believe in the cause, but I believe in men." But the questioning note is lost in the violent events that hurry the novel to its climax; and thereafter John Steinbeck, for all his ardent and admirable humanism, has not sufficiently pursued Doc Burton's anxious insights. Or perhaps he has pursued them in artistically unfruitful directions; for Steinbeck has tended to examine the sociology of the problem and its biology; even, we might say, its physics and its chemistry. He has talked about nodes and nuclei and organisms and cells, wasting his poetic vein on scientific and social-scientific abstractions.

It was during this period that the divergence between Steinbeck and Silone became enlightening; for while *The Grapes of Wrath* (1939) follows a mainly political and sociological course (however emotionally intensified), its counterpart in Silone's career—*Bread and Wine*—registers a defeat of political ambition that is at once a triumph over it, in the name simultaneously of humanity and of art. This is the event acknowledged by Pietro Spina when he tells Luigi Murica that "politics have become somewhat different for us," that the real questions are "What is man? What is this human life?" and the real revolution that of becoming a new human being. It was by thus transcending his political theme that Silone succeeded in truly engaging it, because he was no longer engaged *by* it.

So brief a treatment as this is bound to be unfair to a writer as voluminous, varied, and energetic as Steinbeck. But it seems to me that Steinbeck's writings, from *The Grapes of Wrath* onward, are marked chiefly by the moment and kind of their failure, and for reasons to be hazarded: though in the case at least of *The Grapes of Wrath* of a failure that is in the end almost indistinguishable from success. For *The Grapes of Wrath* is all compact of the themes and qualities we have been everywhere discovering in second-generation fiction. It confirms our sense of what that fiction has aspired to, in its typically creative moments; and even as it fails to fulfill its own aspirations, it reveals, by recompense, the nature of the aim and the requirements for arriving at it. *The Grapes of Wrath* is a picaresque novel in the modern manner, an episodic long tale of encounters along the way of a harried and difficult journey—the journey of dispossessed Oklahomans toward and into the deceptively promising land of California. Steinbeck is at his best as a contriver of episodes, and *The Grapes of Wrath* is crowded with memorable instances of his skill. The hero of the book, Tom Joad, moreover, shares with the heroes of Silone, Camus, and Greene, the contradictory elements that have gone into the contemporary heroic profile: he is something of a criminal, something of a saint, something of a poet. He has killed a man and served some years in jail for doing so; and, as the book concludes, he is an outlaw in that profounder and more saintly sense, a rebel against institutionalized and legalized cruelty, a refugee witness to truth and hence a man—like Pietro Spina and like Graham Greene's Mexican priest—to be hunted down and destroyed. *The Grapes of Wrath* moves to rhythms also sounded by Camus and Silone: it celebrates revolt in the name of human solidarity; the essence of its rebellion is the assertion that "we are." Its angry, personal, conversational tone anticipates with no less eloquence the more severe formulations of Camus in *The Rebel*:

> One man, one family driven from the land [it is Steinbeck's voice, in chapter fourteen]. . . . I am alone and I am bewildered. And in the night one family camps in the ditch and another family pulls in and the tents come out. The two men squat on their hams and the

women and children listen. Here is the node, you who hate change and fear revolution. Keep these two squatting men apart; make them hate, fear, suspect each other. Here is the anlage of the thing you fear. This is the zygote. For here "I lost my land" is changed; a cell is split and from its splitting grows the things you hate—"We lost *our* land." The danger is here, for two men are not as lonely and perplexed as one. And from this "we" there grows a still more dangerous thing: "I have a little food" plus "I have none." If from this problem the sum is "We have a little food," the thing is on its way. . . . This is the beginning—from "I" to "we."

There is no more compassionate paragraph in American fiction; and yet the seeds of artistic defeat are in it. One sign of them is the names given the human relation: node, anlage, zygote; for it is a sign of abstraction at the instant when the human demand is most intense. Steinbeck's quasi-scientific interests seem to have prevented him from focusing on the elements that make up the human relation: sharply outlined and inviolable single persons. He has somehow missed the truth lying behind Martin Buber's insistence that distance (or "distancing," as Buber more actively describes it) is a prerequisite of relationship; and in missing it, Steinbeck has reversed a failure noted earlier in Camus. The distance between persons in *The Plague* remained, psychologically and metaphorically, too large (though, as I have said, this is not so much Camus's failure as a failure in the world he accurately represents); but in Steinbeck, the distance is apt to be too slight for visibility. Steinbeck has always suffered from this: "You have never known a person," the hero of *To a God Unknown* (1933) is told by his sister-in-law; and we feel it is Steinbeck admonishing himself. "You aren't aware of persons . . . only people."

Steinbeck's characters, as a result, tend not to be related but to melt into one another. And they seem to want so to melt, rather than to commune: a recurring danger of individualism, as against another viewpoint that we may perhaps call personalism. *The Grapes of Wrath*, indeed, crowns the Steinbeckian evolution from uniting to melting by associating the latter with the metaphysical doctrine—borrowed from Emerson and introduced into the book by the ex-preacher Jim Casy—of the "oversoul," the doctrine of the one vast transcendent soul of humanity of which each individual has his small particular fragment. "Maybe all men got one big soul and evr'body's a part of it," says Casy; and Tom Joad, his disciple, echoes the notion later, in the much-quoted address to his mother: "A fella ain't got a soul of his own, but on'y a piece of a big one." The big one was rent asunder, in Steinbeck's version of the fall of man and the loss of Eden, by the force of the individual acquisitive instinct; and the effort of men—the novel implies—is not merely to unite, but to restore the primal cosmic unity.

The doctrine of the oversoul, which is a doubtful contribution to political revolt, is also little short of disastrous for fiction; for fiction depends upon the idea that a fellow *does* have a soul of his own, and it often dramatizes historic conditions that seek to deny the fact. But mention of Emerson brings us closer to the nub of Steinbeck's difficulties; for Steinbeck has absorbed both too much and too little of Emerson. While saluting again, in colloquial language, the Emersonian oversoul, Steinbeck overlooked the constant insistence of Emerson upon the irreducible reality of the single person—the insistence in the essay "New England Reformers," for example, that human unity "is only perfect when all the uniters are isolated"; that "it is the union of friends who live in different streets and towns." But the ultimate cause of the honorable kind of failure I am attributing to Steinbeck is exactly an excess of the most characteristic Emersonian spirit: a zestful and insufficiently examined confidence in human nature; and thus an absence of the tragic and ironic spirit with which Steinbeck's contemporary, William Faulkner, is so richly endowed. The tragic spirit, let it be emphasized, is by no means necessary to all writers under all circumstances: for which we may be grateful. But it seems indispensable for a writer of the second generation directly confronting the complex challenges of his time. Steinbeck's work, for example, moves toward an image of what Malraux has called "virile fraternity"; but it does not arrive at the kind of image Malraux offered in his most recent novel—virile fraternity *with the enemy*. There is too indistinct an awareness in Steinbeck that the conventional terms of battle are no longer valid; that the guilt is everywhere and on all sides and in all of us, and the urge to expiate the guilt as well; that the very problem of the problematical novel is nothing less than the nature of man. To have reached that awareness and to have presented it in narrative would not have meant relapsing into the sad and the poignant; for tragedy has little to do with sadness, any more than it has to do with the otherwise healthy anger that, in Steinbeck, is a substitute for the tragic spirit. Nor would it have meant any loss of his appealing, compassionate earthy humor. It would have meant protecting that humor from the sentimentality to which it has often declined. It would have meant transforming it into something a good deal more compelling—what Hawthorne once described as "the tragic power of laughter."

Chronology of Important Dates

1902 JS born February 27 in Salinas, California.

1919 JS graduated from Salinas High School.

1920–25 JS studied English at Stanford University and published in *Stanford Spectator.*

1925 JS left Stanford and went to New York, where he worked as a reporter for the *American.*

1929 *Cup of Gold.*

1930 JS married Carol Henning and moved to Pacific Grove, where he met Edward Ricketts.

1932 *The Pastures of Heaven.*

1933 *To a God Unknown.*

1934 "The Murder" wins O. Henry Prize.

1935 *Tortilla Flat.*

1936 *In Dubious Battle*; "The Harvest Gypsies," series on migrant workers, in *San Francisco News.*

1937 *Of Mice and Men* (novel and play); *The Red Pony* (in three parts).

1938 *The Long Valley; Their Blood Is Strong.*

1939 *The Grapes of Wrath.*

1940 Pulitzer Prize for *The Grapes of Wrath*; film versions of *The Grapes of Wrath* and *Of Mice and Men.*

1941 *Sea of Cortez* (with Edward Ricketts).

1942 *The Moon Is Down* (novel and play); *Bombs Away,* written for Army Air Corps; film of *Tortilla Flat*; JS divorced from Carol Henning.

1943 Married Gwyndolen Conger (Verdon) and moved to New York; JS was war correspondent in Europe for *New York Herald Tribune;* film of *The Moon Is Down.*

1944   JS wrote script for Alfred Hitchcock's *Lifeboat.*

1945   *Cannery Row; The Red Pony* (in four parts); "The Pearl of the World" in *Woman's Home Companion; A Medal for Benny* (film).

1947   *The Wayward Bus; The Pearl* (novel and film).

1948   *A Russian Journal*; JS divorced from Gwyndolen Conger; Ed Ricketts died.

1949   Film of *The Red Pony.*

1950   *Burning Bright* (novel and play); *Viva Zapata!* (film); JS married Elaine Scott.

1951   *Log from the Sea of Cortez.*

1952   *East of Eden;* articles from Europe for *Colliers.*

1954   *Sweet Thursday.*

1955   *Pipe Dream* (Rodgers and Hammerstein musical based on *Sweet Thursday*); film of *East of Eden.*

1957   *The Short Reign of Pippin IV*; film of *The Wayward Bus.*

1958   *Once There Was a War* (collection of war dispatches).

1961   *The Winter of Our Discontent.*

1962   *Travels with Charley in Search of America*; JS won Nobel Prize for literature.

1965   "Letters to Alicia" for *Newsday.*

1966   *America and Americans.*

1968   JS died December 20 and was buried in Salinas.

1969   *Journal of a Novel: The "East of Eden" Letters.*

Notes on the Editor and Contributors

ROBERT CON DAVIS directs the English graduate program at the University of Oklahoma, where he teaches American fiction and critical theory. Recently he edited and contributed to *The Fictional Father: Lacanian Readings of the Text* (University of Massachusetts Press).

EDWIN T. BOWDEN teaches American literature at the University of Texas, Austin. He has published numerous articles and books on American literature and is textual editor of a new scholarly edition of the works of Washington Irving, now appearing volume by volume (Twayne).

WARREN FRENCH, a major Steinbeck scholar, has taught and written about a wide range of topics in American studies. He is chair of the American Studies Department at Indiana University/Purdue University at Indianapolis.

J. PAUL HUNTER, former chair of the Department of English at Emory University, has written on eighteenth-century British fiction and on many aspects of British and American studies. Among his books is *The Reluctant Pilgrim,* a study of *Robinson Crusoe* (Johns Hopkins University Press).

PETER LISCA is a major Steinbeck scholar and has done much to establish the direction of Steinbeck research. He recently published *John Steinbeck: Nature and Myth* (Thomas Y. Crowell). He teaches at the University of Florida.

LEONARD LUTWACK teaches American literature at the University of Maryland, College Park. He has published widely on nineteenth- and twentieth-century American literature and has just completed a study of "place in literature."

GEORGE BLUESTONE is a writer/producer of films as well as a scholar of film studies. He has done several books and feature films (including MGM's *The Walking Stick*). Since 1972 he has been Professor of Film at Boston University.

STUART L. BURNS teaches twentieth-century American literature at Drake

University in Des Moines, Iowa. Most recently, he published *Whores Before Descartes: Assorted Prose and Poetry* (Launderen Press).

MARY ELLEN CALDWELL is an Emeritus Professor at the University of North Dakota. She writes on and teaches American literature, mainly of the nineteenth century.

ROBERT J. GRIFFIN has taught at Yale and California State University and has published numerous essays on English and American literature. He is now Executive Secretary of the Council of University of California Faculty Associations.

WILLIAM A. FREEDMAN has published many essays on English and American literature. He has taught at the University of Chicago and now teaches at Haifa University in Israel.

HORST GROENE is Senior Lecturer in English at Kiel University. In addition to his work on Steinbeck, he has published widely on American writers such as Sherwood Anderson, J. D. Salinger, and Tennessee Williams.

JOAN HEDRICK has taught English and American studies at Wesleyan University. She has written several articles on American social history in the Gilded Age. Most recently she published *Solitary Comrade: Jack London and His Work* (University of North Carolina Press).

R.W.B. LEWIS teaches at Yale University and is a distinguished scholar of American literature. Two of his books are *The American Adam* (University of Chicago Press) and *Edith Wharton: A Biography* (Harper).

Selected Bibliography

Editions

Although there is no definitive, scholarly edition of *The Grapes of Wrath*, several editions by Viking Press are generally reliable and inexpensive. Among those is the "Critical Edition" by Peter Lisca (1972), a convenient text and collection of criticism.

Commentaries

Major commentaries on *The Grapes of Wrath* are referred to in the Introduction and in the essays in this volume. The following list is a representative sampling of other useful studies of the novel.

Benson, Jackson J. " 'To Tom, Who Lived It': John Steinbeck and the Man from Weedpatch." *Journal of Modern Literature*, 5 (1976):151–94.

Berry, J. Wilkes. "Enduring Life in *The Grapes of Wrath*." *CEA Critic,* 33, 2 (1971):18–19.

Brasch, James D. "*The Grapes of Wrath* and Old Testament Skepticism." *San Jose Studies,* 3, 2 (1977):16–27.

Bredalh, A. Carl, Jr. "The Drinking Metaphor in *The Grapes of Wrath*." *Steinbeck Quarterly,* 6 (Fall 1973):95–98.

Campbell, Russell. "Trampling Out the Vintage: Sour Grapes," in Gerald Peary and Roger Shatzkin, eds., *The Modern American Novel and the Movies* (Ungar Film Library). New York: Ungar, 1978, pp. 107–18.

Carr, Duane R. "Steinbeck's Blakean Vision in *The Grapes of Wrath*." *Steinbeck Quarterly,* 8 (Summer–Fall 1975):67–73.

Caselli, Jaclyn R. "John Steinbeck and the American Patchwork Quilt." *San Jose Studies,* 1, 3 (1975):83–87.

Collins, Thomas A. "From *Bringing in the Sheaves*," with a Foreword by John Steinbeck. *Journal of Modern Literature,* 5 (1976): 211–32.

Covici, Pascal, Jr. "From Commitment to Choice: Double Vision and the Problem of Vitality from John Steinbeck," in Warren French, ed., *The Fifties: Fiction, Poetry, Drama* (with Introd.). Deland, Fla.: Everett/ Edwards, 1970, pp. 63–71.

Cox, Martha Heasley. "The Conclusion of *The Grapes of Wrath:* Steinbeck's Conception and Execution." *San Jose Studies,* 1, 3 (1975): 73–81.

——. "Fact into Fiction in *The Grapes of Wrath:* The Weedpatch and Arvin Camps," in Tetsumaro Hayashi, Yasuo Hashiguichi, and Richard F. Peterson, eds., *John Steinbeck: East and West.* Muncie, Ind.: Steinbeck Society of America, English Department, Ball State University, 1978. (Introd. by Warren French, pp. 12–21.)

Davis, Robert Murray. *Steinbeck: A Collection of Critical Essays* (with Introd.). Englewood Cliffs, N.J.: Prentice-Hall, 1972.

Ditsky, John. "The Ending of *The Grapes of Wrath:* A Further Commentary." *Agora,* 2, 2 (1973):41–50.

——. "*The Grapes of Wrath:* A Reconsideration." *Southern Humanities Review,* 13 (1979):215–20.

Donohue, Agnes M., ed., *A Casebook on "The Grapes of Wrath."* New York: Thomas Y. Crowell, 1968.

Fossey, W. Richard. "The End of the Western Dream: *The Grapes of Wrath* and Oklahoma." *Cimarron Review,* 22 (1973):25–34.

French, Warren. "After *The Grapes of Wrath.*" *Steinbeck Quarterly,* 8 (Summer–Fall 1975):73–78.

——. *A Companion to "The Grapes of Wrath."* New York: The Viking Press, 1963. Now a little dated, this book is still a useful guide for background on the novel; also discusses important special topics.

——. "John Steinbeck and Modernism," in Tetsumaro Hayashi and Kenneth D. Swan, eds., *Steinbeck's Prophetic Vision of America: Proceedings of the Bicentennial Steinbeck Seminar.* Upland, Ind.: Taylor University for Steinbeck Society of America, 1976, pp. 35–55.

——. *The Social Novel at the End of an Era.* Carbondale: Southern Illinois University Press, 1966, pp. 42–86.

——. "Steinbeck's *The Grapes of Wrath* (1939)," in Tetsumaro Hayashi, ed., *A Study Guide to Steinbeck: A Handbook to His Major Works.* Metuchen, N.J.: Scarecrow, 1974.

Gurko, Leo. *The Angry Decade.* New York: Dodd, Mead, 1947.

Haeberle, Erwin J. "Steinbeck: *The Grapes of Wrath*," in Hans-Joachim Lang, ed., *Der Amerikanische Roman: Von den Anfangen bis zur Gegenwart.* Dusseldorf: August Bael, 1972, pp. 301–32.

Hayashi, Tetsumaro. "Steinbeck's Women in *The Grapes of Wrath*: A New Perspective." *Kyushu American Literature,* 18 (October 1977):1–4.

Jain, Sunita. "The Concept of Man in the Novels of John Steinbeck." *Journal of the School of Languages,* 3, 1 (1975):98–102.

———. *John Steinbeck's Concept of Man: A Critical Study of His Novels.* New Delhi: New Statesman, 1979.

Kallapur, S. T. "*The Grapes of Wrath*: A Reevaluation," in M. K. Naik, S. K. Desai, and S. Mokashi-Punekar, eds., *Indian Studies in American Fiction.* Dharwar: Karnatak University, Delhi: Macmillan India, 1974.

Kiernan, Thomas. *The Intricate Music: A Biography of John Steinbeck.* Boston: Little, Brown, 1979.

Lieber, Todd M. "Talismanic Patterns in the Novels of John Steinbeck." *American Literature,* 44 (1972): 262–75.

Lisca, Peter. "The Dynamics of Community in *The Grapes of Wrath*," in Motley Deakin and Peter Lisca, eds., *From Irving to Steinbeck: Studies of American Literature in Honor of Harry R. Warfel.* Gainesville: University of Florida Press, 1972.

———. *The Wide World of John Steinbeck.* New Brunswick, N.J.: Rutgers University Press, 1958.

Matton, Collin G. "Water Imagery and the Conclusion to *The Grapes of Wrath*." *A Publication of the Northeast Modern Language Association, Newsletter,* 2 (1970):44–47.

Mendelson, Maurice. "From *The Grapes of Wrath* to *The Winter of Our Discontent*," in Ronald Vroon, trans., *Twentieth-Century American Literature: A Soviet View.* Moscow: Progress, 1976, pp. 411–26.

Otus-Basket, Belma. "Toplumsal Değişimi Yansitan Romanlar Olarak *Ince* Memed ve Gazap Üzümleri." *Bati Edebiyatlari Arastirma Dergisi* (Ankara, Turkey), 1 (1979): 68–75. Yaşar Kemal's *Memed My Hawk* and *The Grapes of Wrath* as novels of change.

Pizer, Donald. "John Steinbeck and American Naturalism." *Steinbeck Quarterly,* 9 (Winter 1976):12–15.

Simmonds, Roy S. *Steinbeck's Literary Achievement.* Muncie, Ind.: Ball State University, 1976.

Tedlock, E. W., Jr., and C. V. Wicker. *Steinbeck and His Critics.* Albuquerque: University of New Mexico Press, 1965. This collection is now dated, but it is a landmark attempt to bring serious critical attention to Steinbeck's work. Also, Steinbeck knew of and seemed greatly interested in this book.

Watkins, Floyd C. "Flat Wine from *The Grapes of Wrath*," in Barbara W. Bitter and Frederick K. Sanders, ed., *The Humanist in His World: Essays in Honor of Fielding Dillard Russell.* Greenwood, S.C.: Attic, 1976.

Yano, Shigeharu. "*The Grapes of Wrath*: The Symbol of Eternity." *Reitaku University Quarterly,* 23 (July 1977):35–37.

Zollman, Sol. "John Steinbeck's Political Outlook in *The Grapes of Wrath*." *Literature and Ideology* (Montreal), 13 (1972):9–20.